# NORFOLK
# IN PHOTOGRAPHS

## JAMIE SKIPPER

AMBERLEY

First published 2018

Amberley Publishing
The Hill, Stroud
Gloucestershire, GL5 4EP

www.amberley-books.com

Copyright © Jamie Skipper, 2018

The right of Jamie Skipper to be identified as the Author of this work has been
asserted in accordance with the Copyrights, Designs and Patents Act 1988.

ISBN 978 1 4456 7562 6 (print)
ISBN 978 1 4456 7563 3 (ebook)

British Library Cataloguing in Publication Data.
A catalogue record for this book is available from the British Library.

Origination by Amberley Publishing.
Printed in the UK.

# ABOUT THE AUTHOR

Jamie Skipper is a self-taught hobbyist photographer born and bred in the lovely county of Norfolk where much of his landscape photography is based. While most people are still in bed he waits for the exquisite light that only the golden hours of dawn and dusk can produce – beautiful oranges, blues, pinks and purples – lost in the full sunlight of the later day ahead. These can be fully appreciated in the remote landscapes around the county, with only the birds singing, deer and foxes roaming the countryside and (if he's lucky) a barn owl silently quartering a meadow for company, making for a peaceful, relaxing experience far away from the bustle of everyday life.

Using exclusively Canon gear, he started in the relatively distant past with a film Canon EOS 55 ON and worked through several digital models. He currently uses Canon's full frame EOS 6D with a range of their 'L' lenses, which perform very well and will last for years. He also uses several filters and his favourite is the '10 stop' filter that turns even daylight shots into dramatic cloud-blurring long exposures that really transform the image.

Website: www.jdsphoto.co.uk
Twitter: @JDS9_Photo
Facebook: JamieSkipperPhotography

# ACKNOWLEDGEMENTS

I'd like to thank my mum Jan for all the encouragement and support through the years; my late father Phillip, from whom I gained my love of photography; my brother Chris, who shares my interest in photography and is a talented photographer himself; and also my older brother Gary.

Thanks must go to my great friend Marisha Haylett, who has always got good things to say about my work, even when I'm not so sure.

Thanks also to Marcus Tilsley, who talked me into going ahead with the book at the start, and Rod Gowen, a real Norfolk gem whose knowledge of the Norfolk Broads has been invaluable and inspirational, and I'd better not leave out Owen Gedge.

At Amberley Publishing, thanks to Alan Murphy, who saw my work and gave me the opportunity to produce this book, also to Jenny Stephens for the help with the process and Marcus Pennington, my editor.

Thanks also to all my followers past, present and, hopefully, future on Flickr, Twitter and Facebook, whose likes, comments and follows are very much appreciated.

# INTRODUCTION

Wherever you go in Norfolk the landscape changes; there are no mountains, no vast lakes or large metropolitan areas like other parts of the UK, but the diverse and quite unique rural landscape of Norfolk ranges from the modest hills of North Norfolk and the vast flat wetlands of the Broads National Park in the east to the large forested area in the south-west. There are small quaint villages, historic market towns where life continues as it has for countless years, and the beautiful medieval city of Norwich with its ancient streets and picturesque buildings, two stunning cathedrals and a castle on a hill – one can get lost in its winding narrow streets full of character and history.

The fabulous Norfolk coast is famous for its unspoilt stretches of vast clean beaches and lovely resorts like Yarmouth, Cromer and Hunstanton and numerous nature reserves at Cley, Titchwell and Snettisham, as well as wildlife havens at Winterton and Blakeney to name but a few.

However, what Norfolk is probably most famous for is the one-of-a-kind Norfolk Broads National Park, a man-made environment of stunning and peaceful beauty, rivers, waterways, reed beds and broads bursting with wildlife – many rare and unique species calling it home – quaint villages, many cottages thatched with local reeds and the ubiquitous windmills dotting the horizon, giving a feeling of a more relaxed bygone time.

This book, I hope, shows some of the highlights of this wonderful county, a place you can explore with or without a camera and enjoy all it has to offer. Whether it's a cool misty morning on the Broads or a beautiful vast sunset in Norfolk's big skies, I guarantee it'll leave an impression on you for all time.

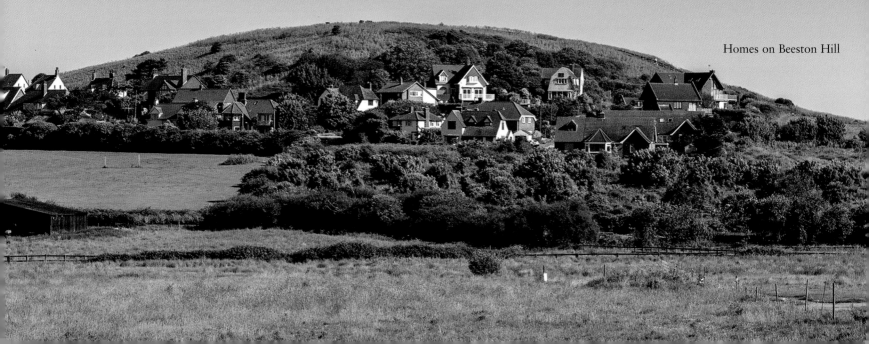

Homes on Beeston Hill

# AROUND NORFOLK

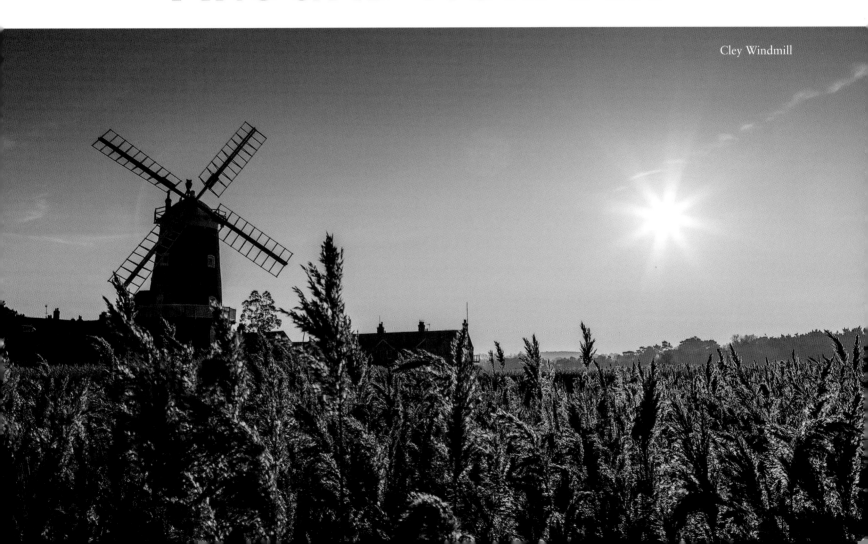

Cley Windmill

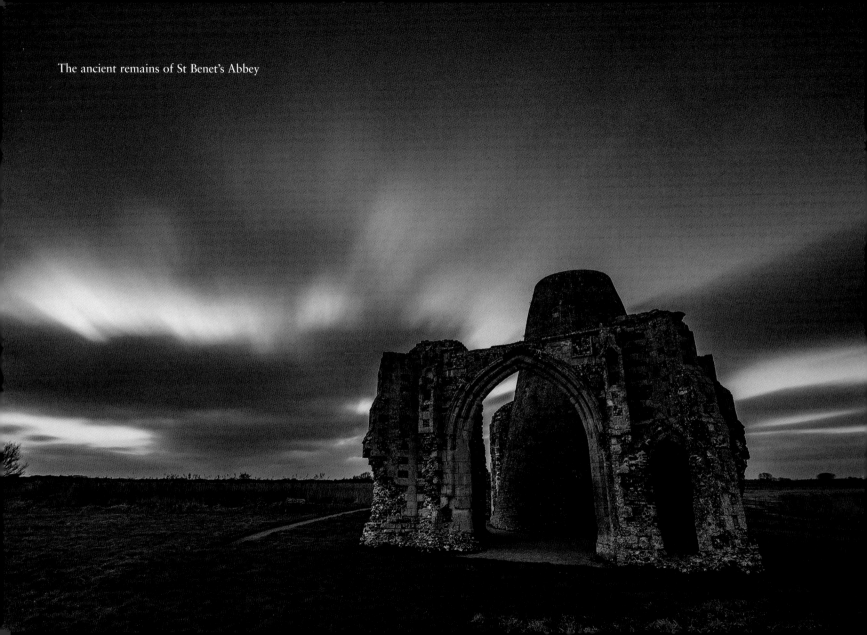

The ancient remains of St Benet's Abbey

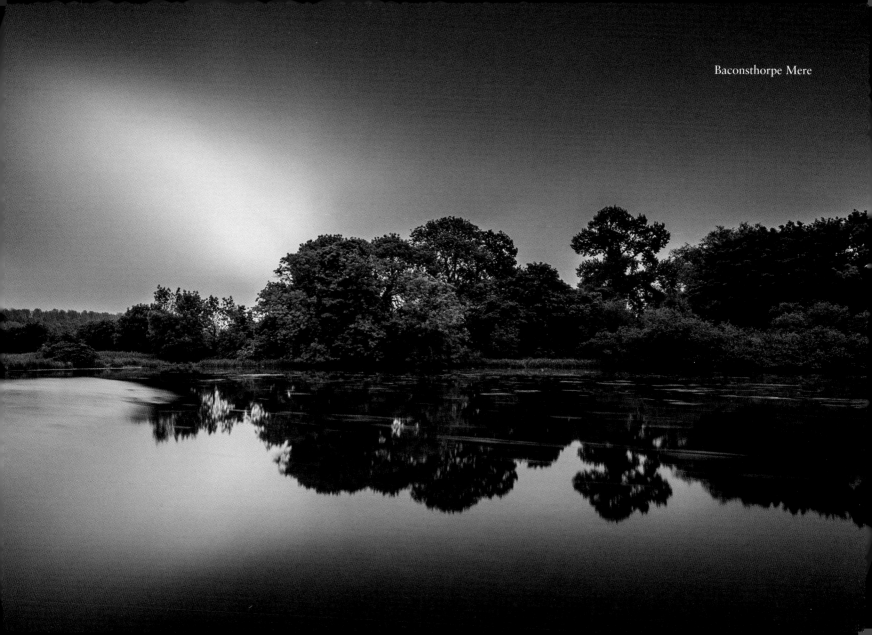

Baconsthorpe Mere

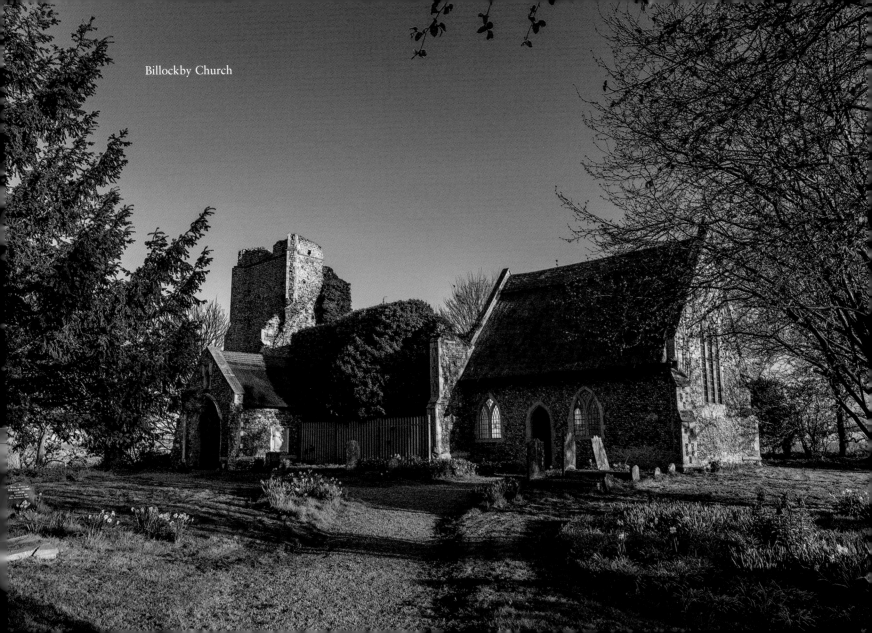

Billockby Church

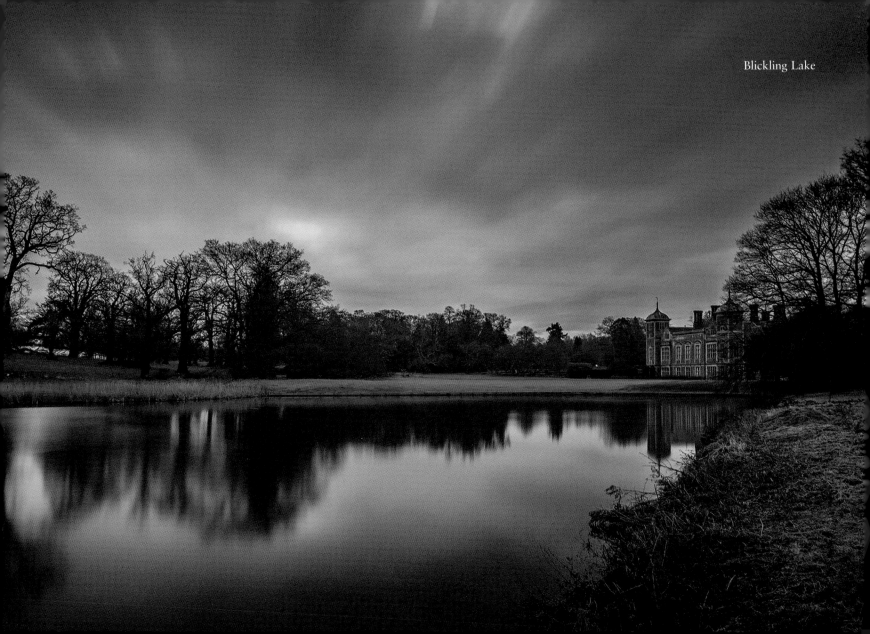

Blickling Lake

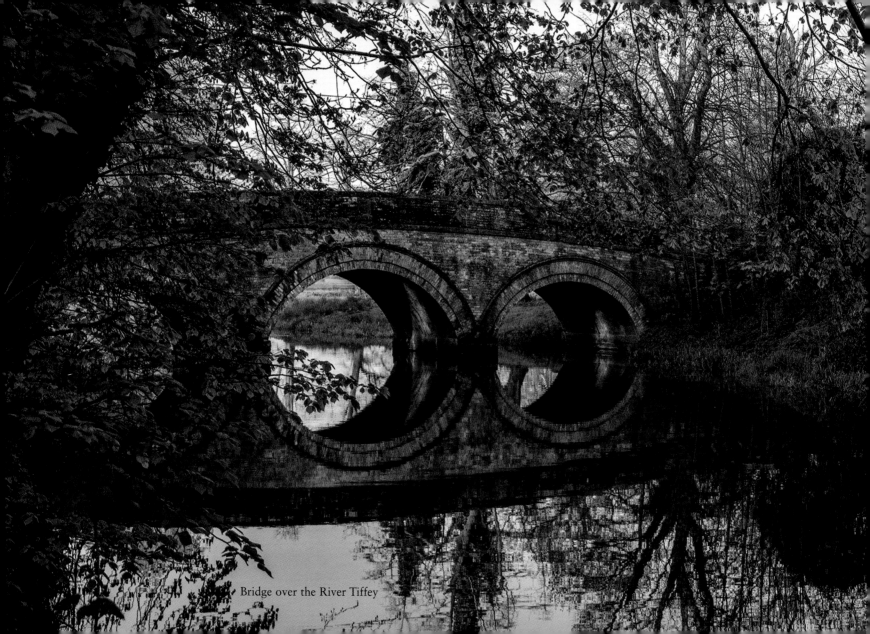

Bridge over the River Tiffey

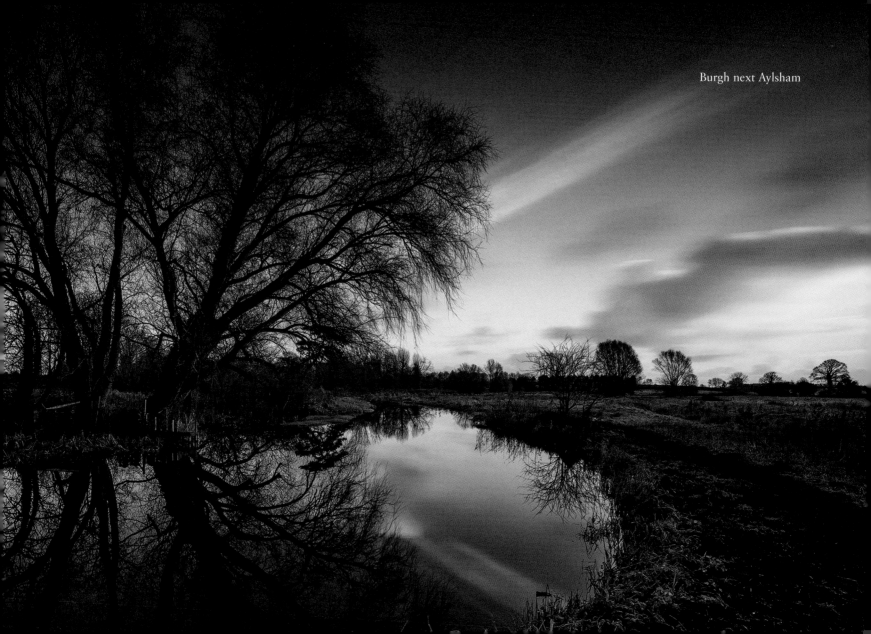

Burgh next Aylsham

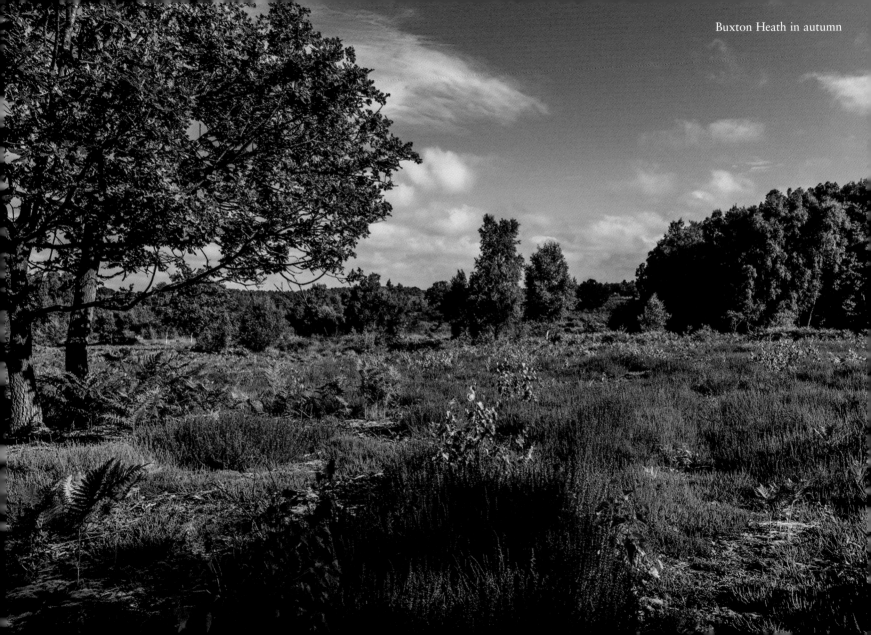

Buxton Heath in autumn

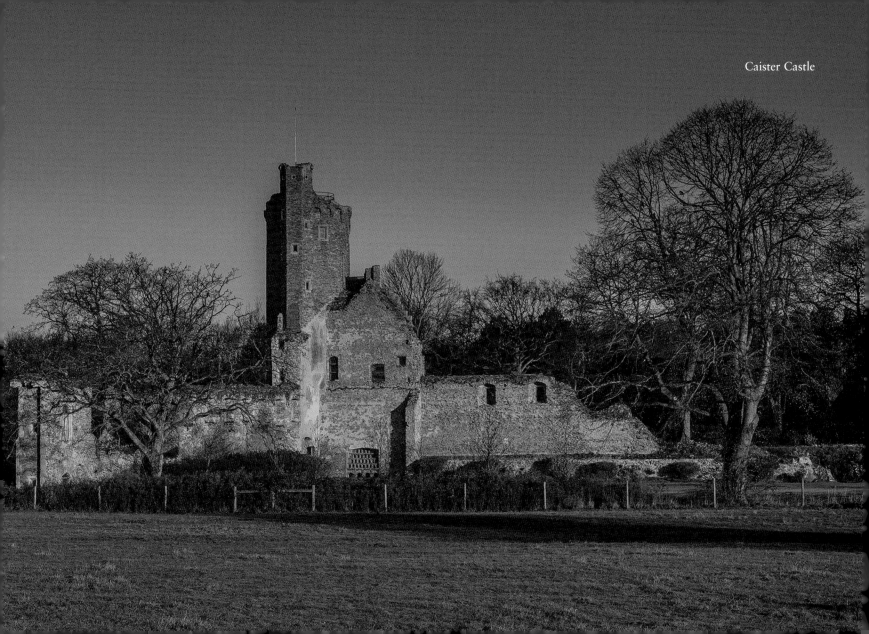

Caister Castle

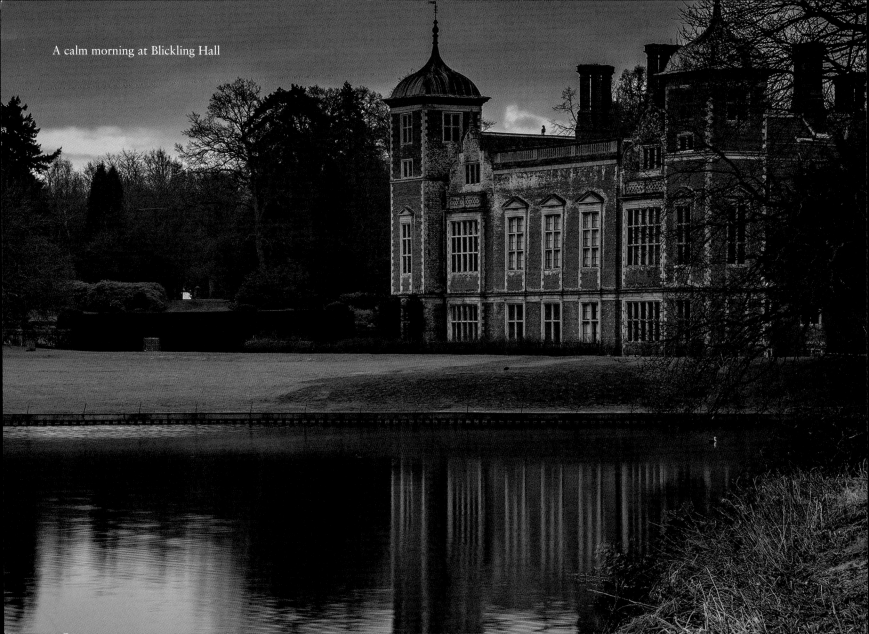

A calm morning at Blickling Hall

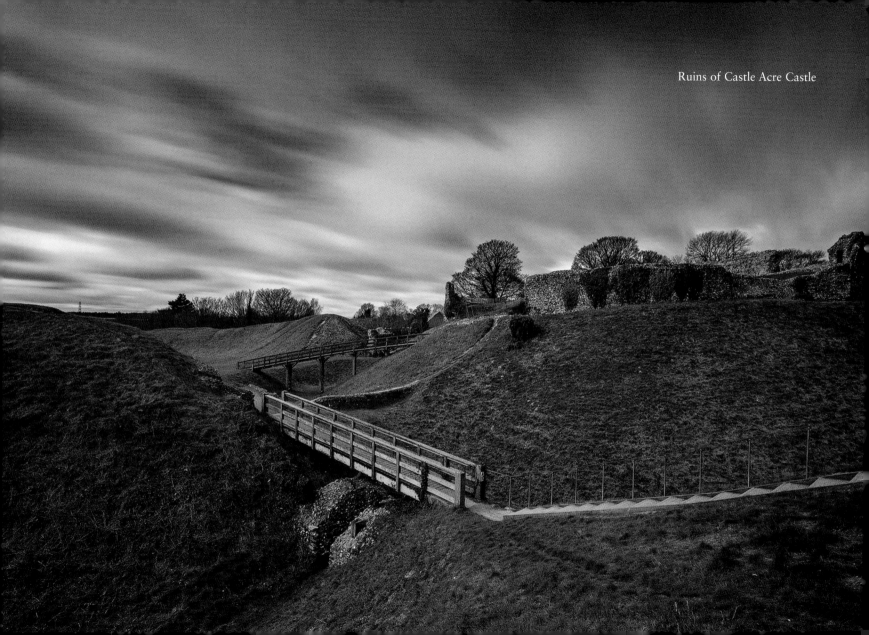

Ruins of Castle Acre Castle

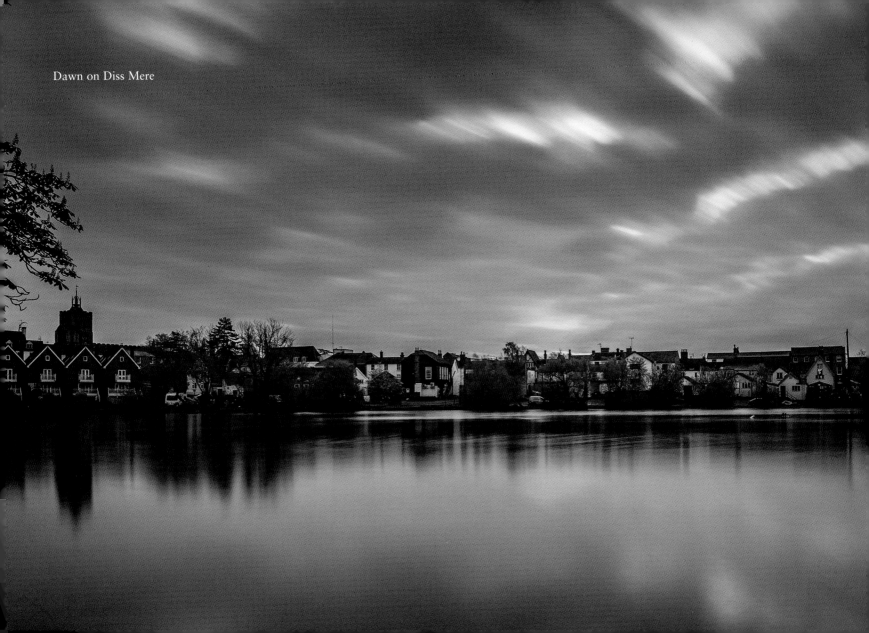

Dawn on Diss Mere

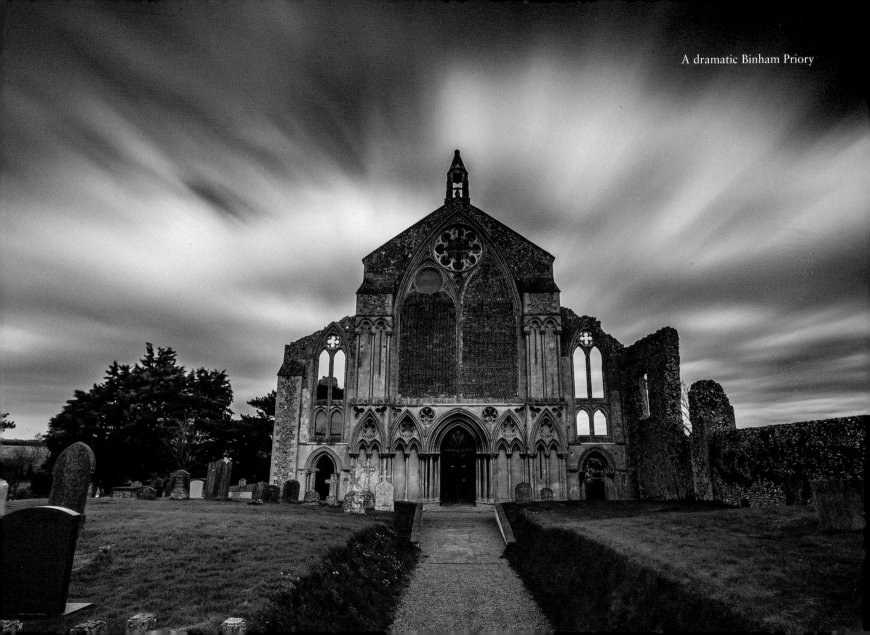

A dramatic Binham Priory

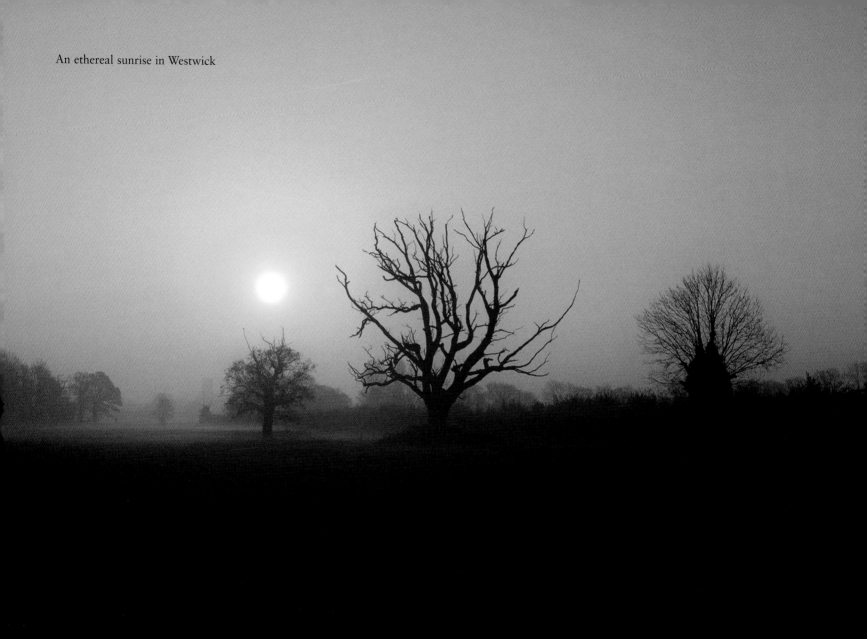

An ethereal sunrise in Westwick

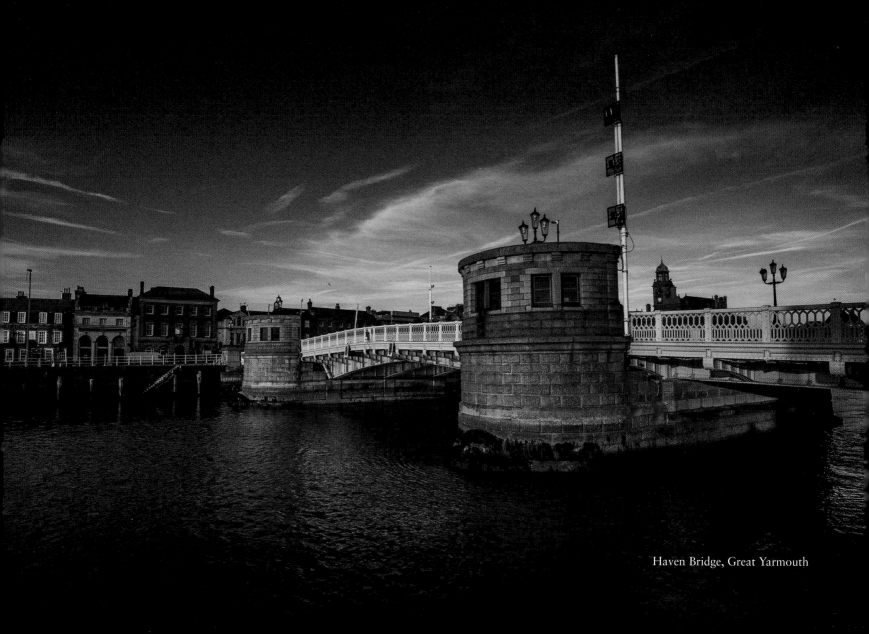

Haven Bridge, Great Yarmouth

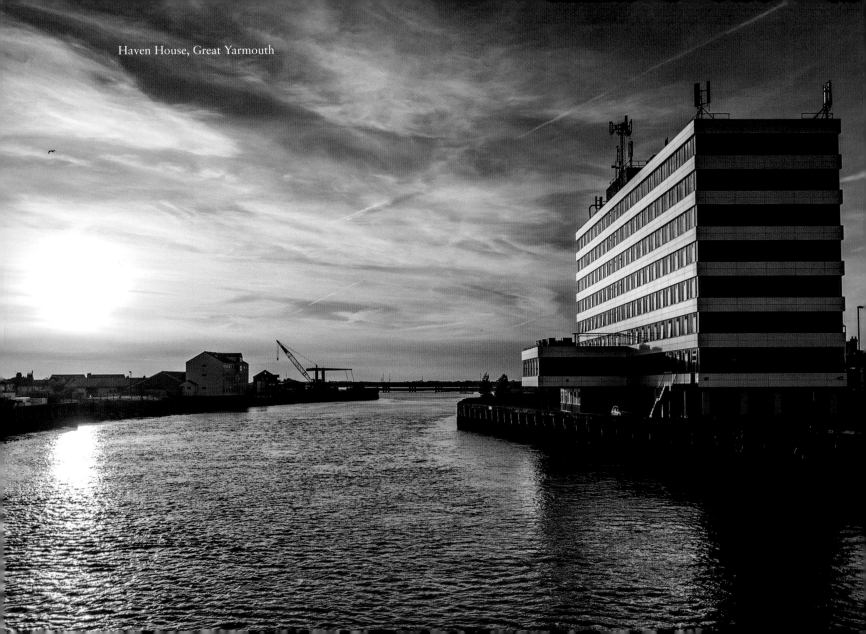

Haven House, Great Yarmouth

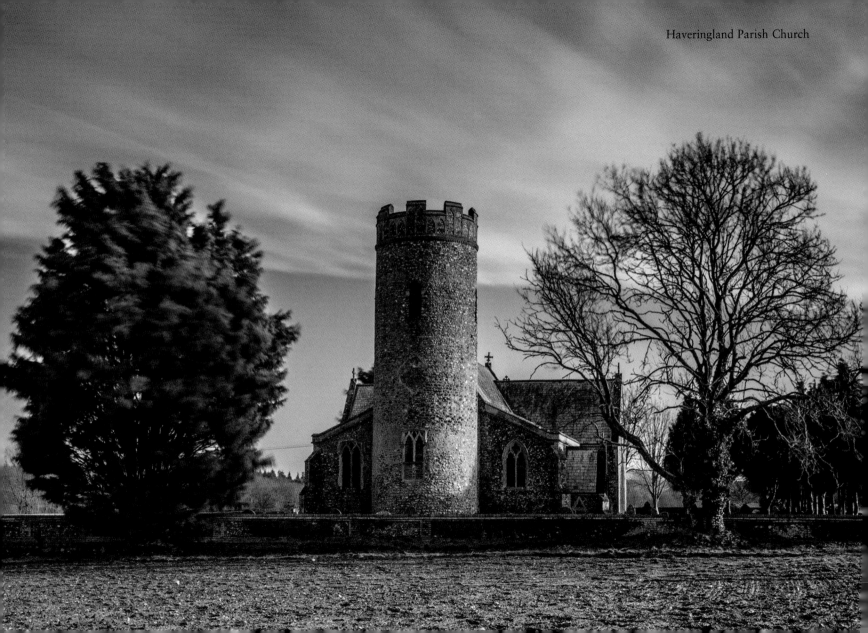

Haveringland Parish Church

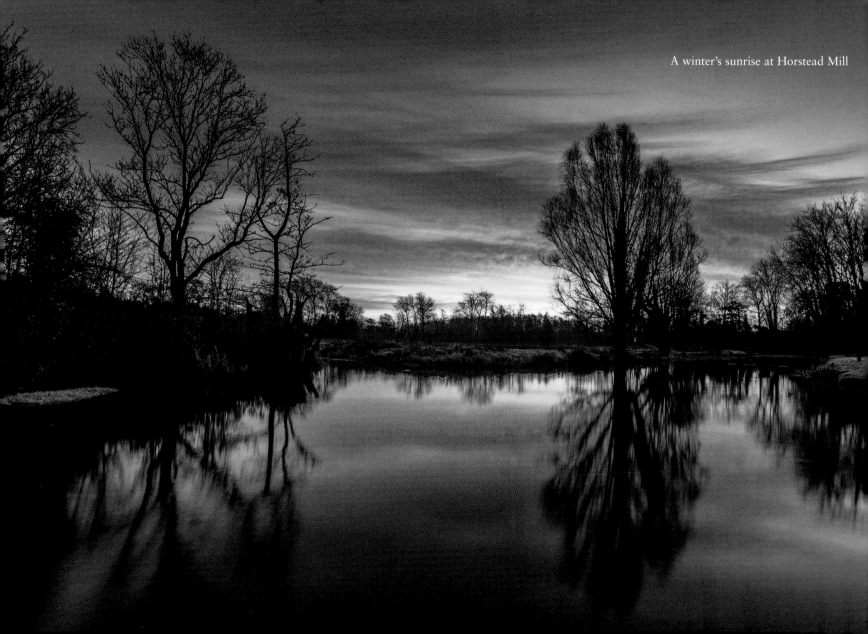
A winter's sunrise at Horstead Mill

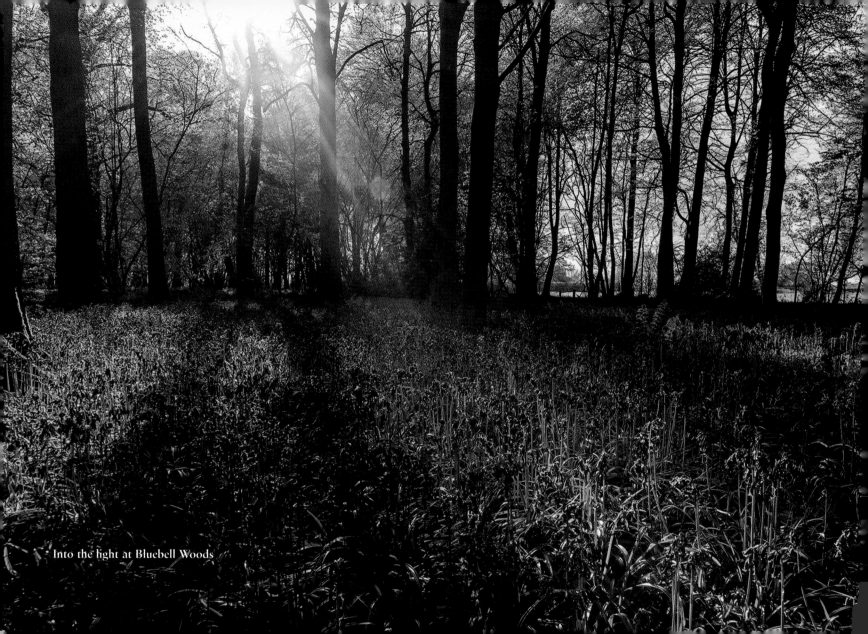

Into the light at Bluebell Woods

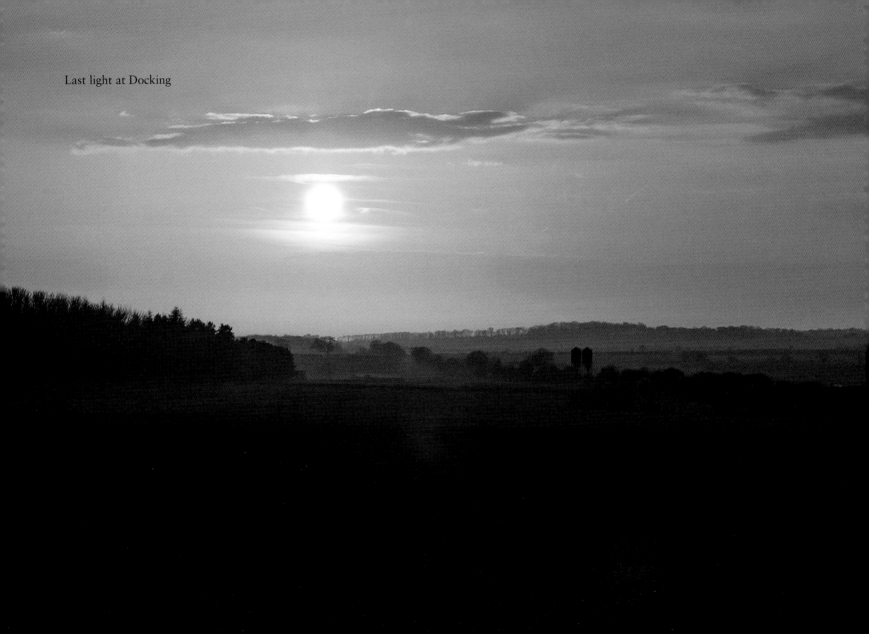
Last light at Docking

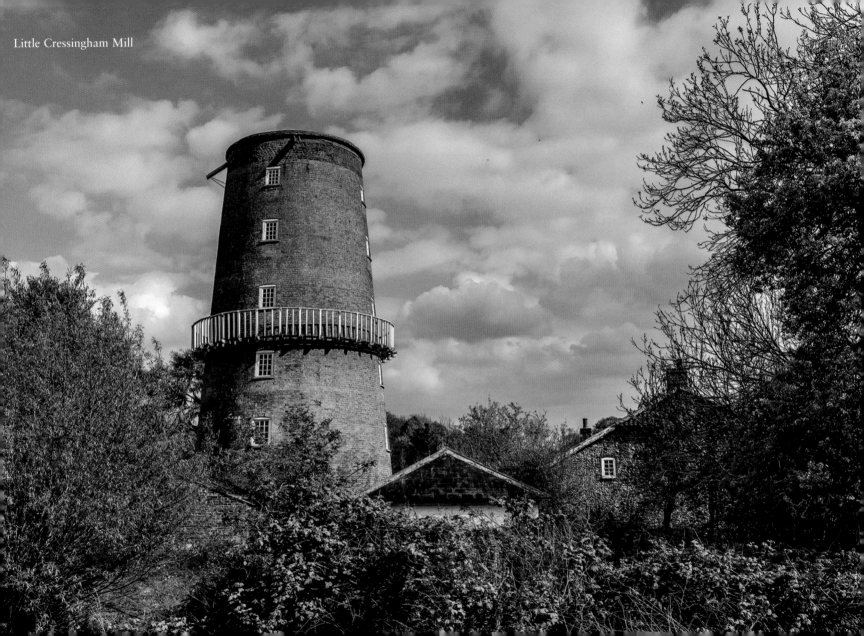

Little Cressingham Mill

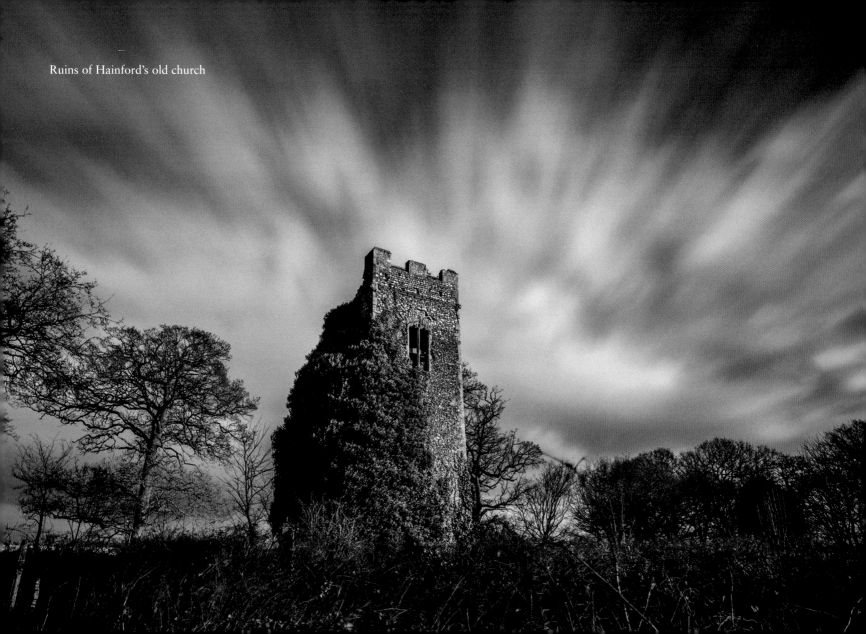

Ruins of Hainford's old church

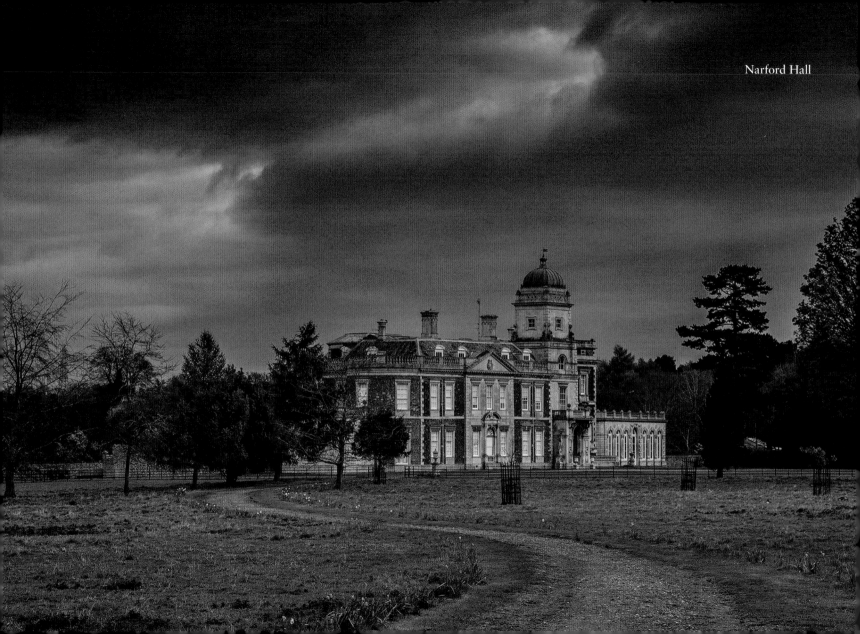

Narford Hall

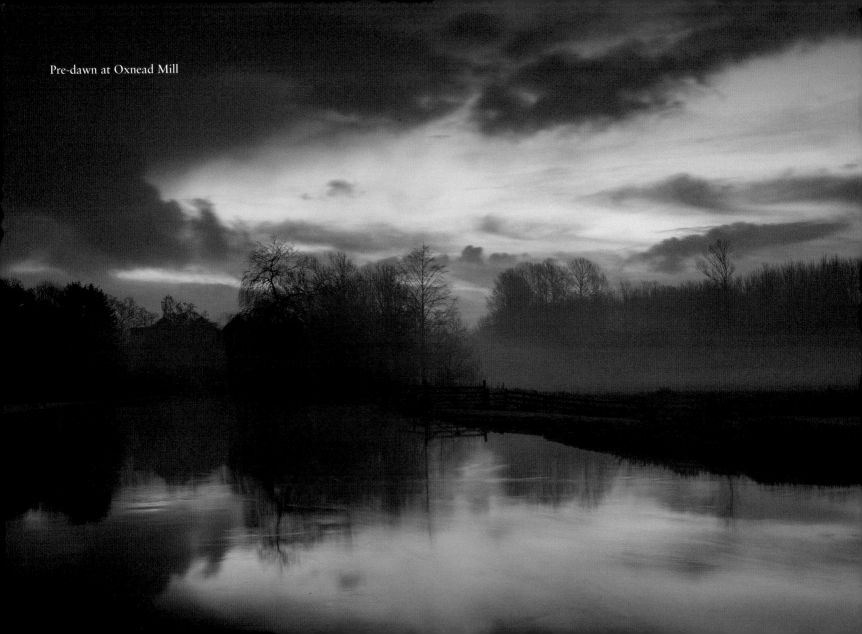

Pre-dawn at Oxnead Mill

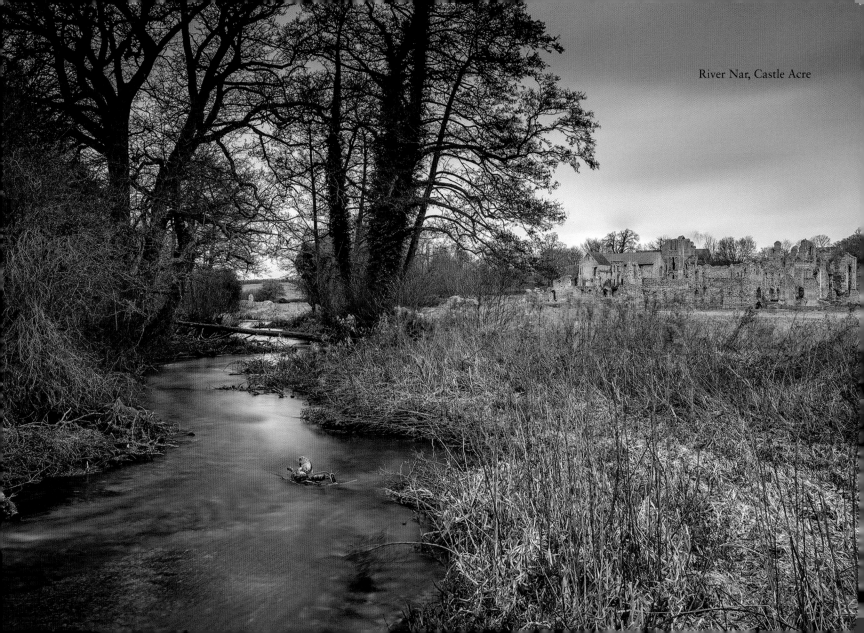

River Nar, Castle Acre

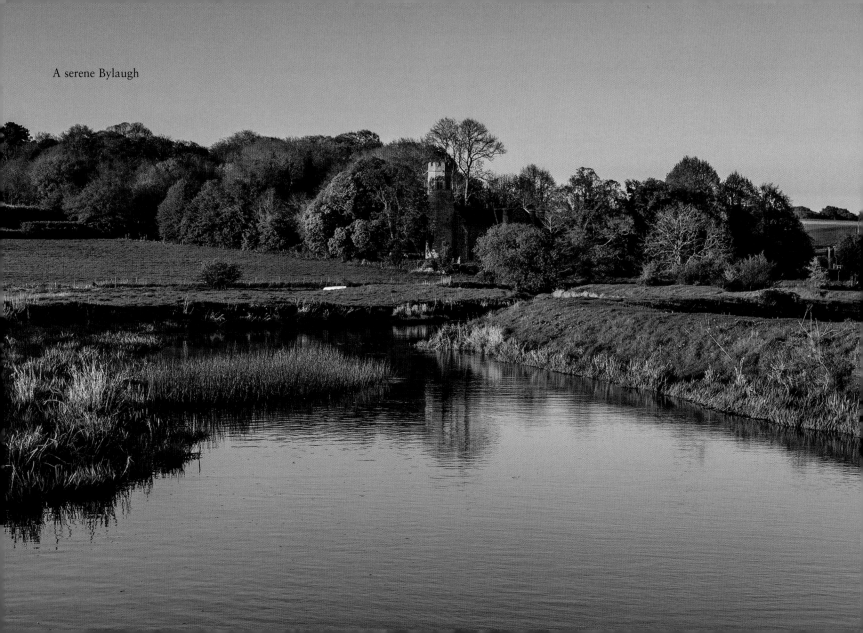

A serene Bylaugh

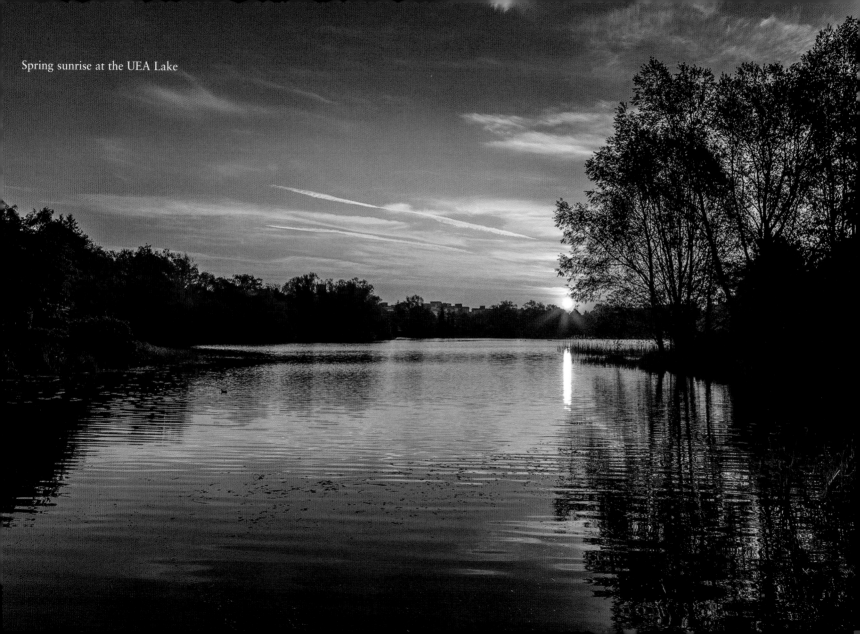

Spring sunrise at the UEA Lake

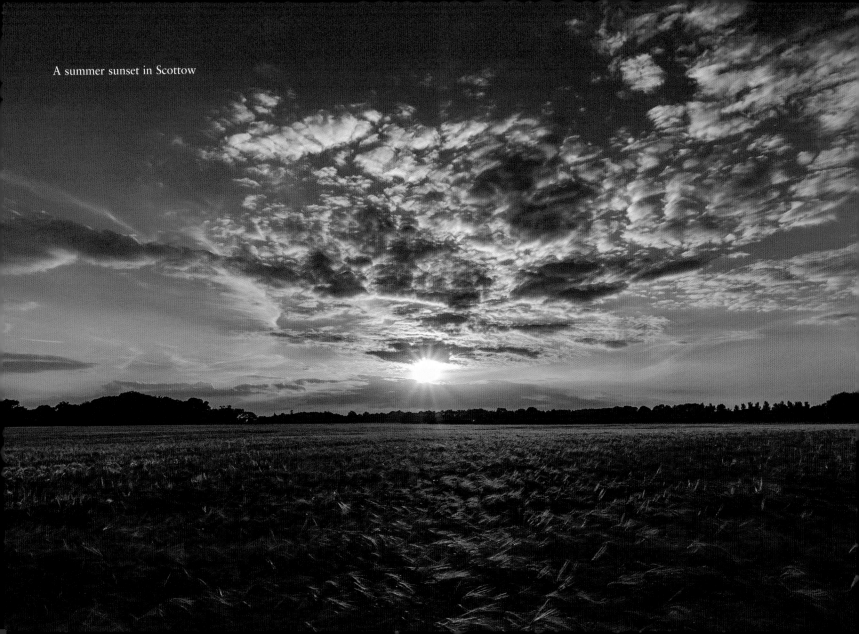
A summer sunset in Scottow

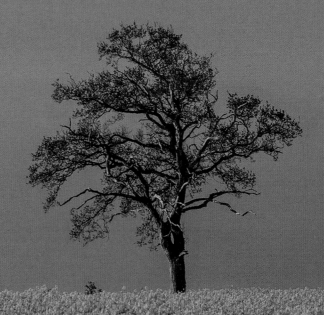

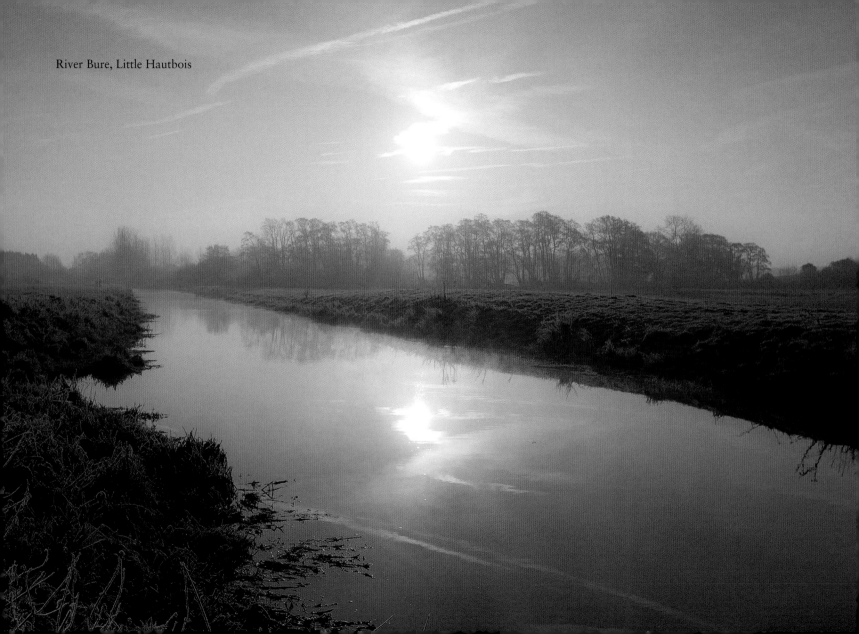

River Bure, Little Hautbois

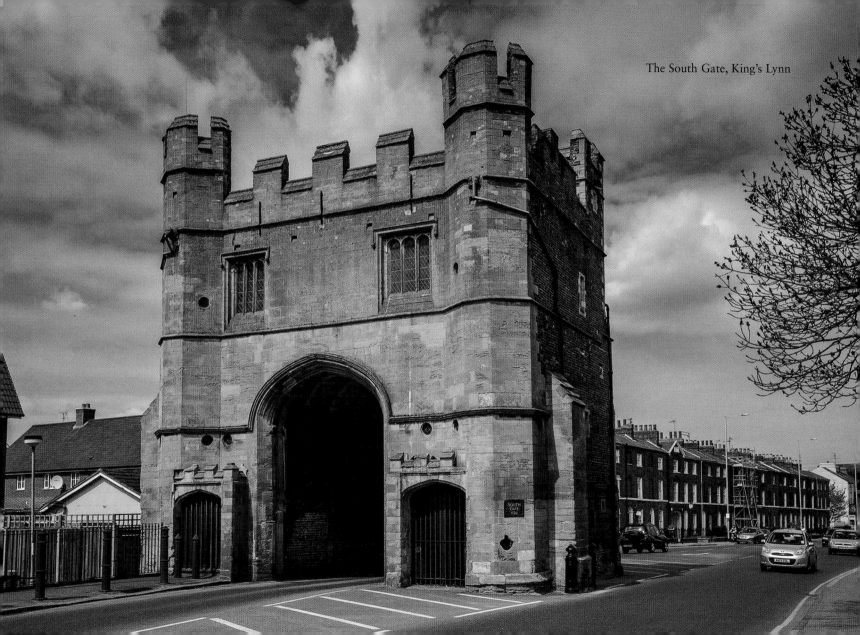

The South Gate, King's Lynn

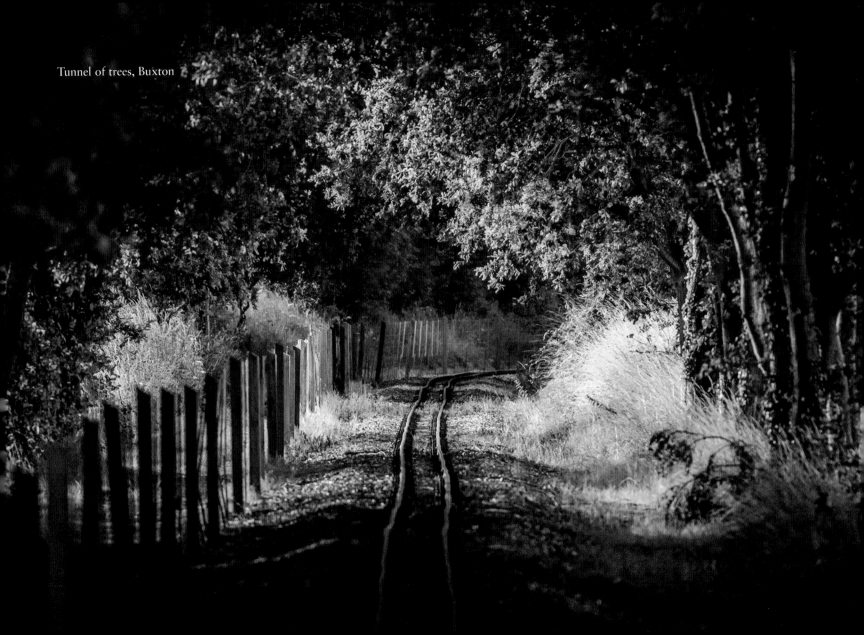

Tunnel of trees, Buxton

# COASTAL NORFOLK

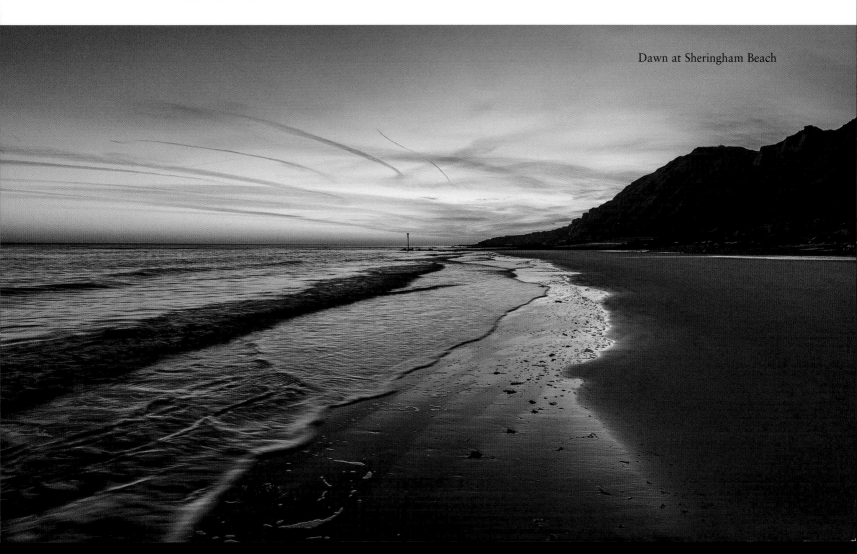

Dawn at Sheringham Beach

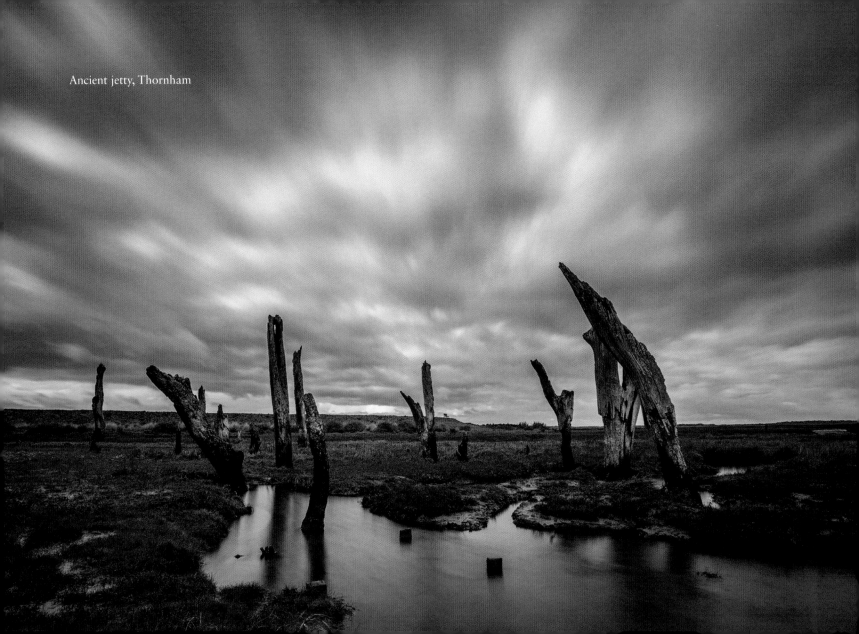
Ancient jetty, Thornham

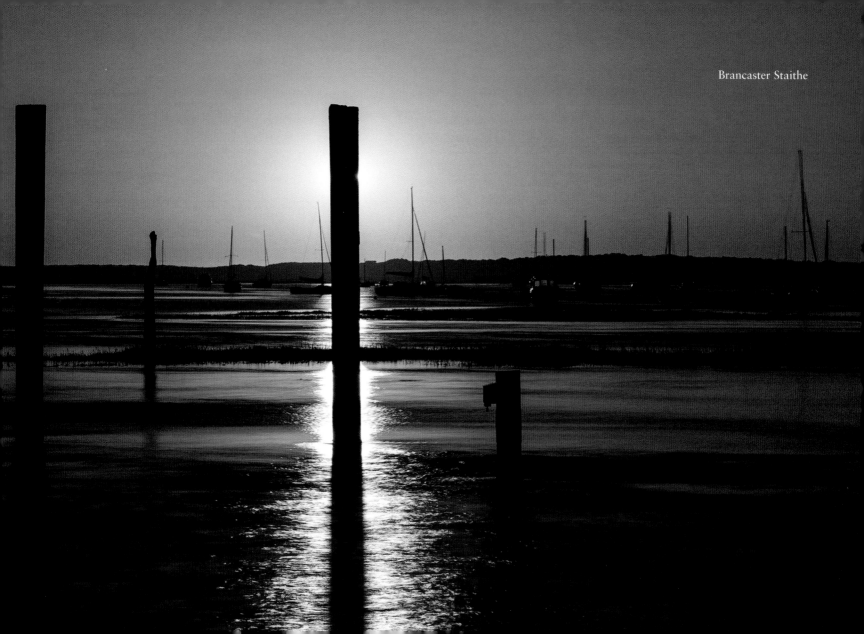

Brancaster Staithe

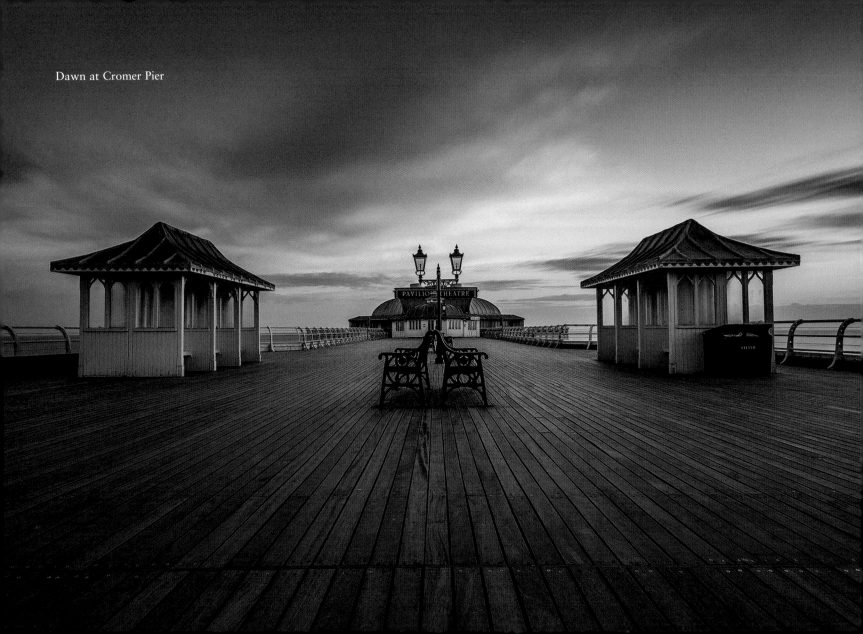

Dawn at Cromer Pier

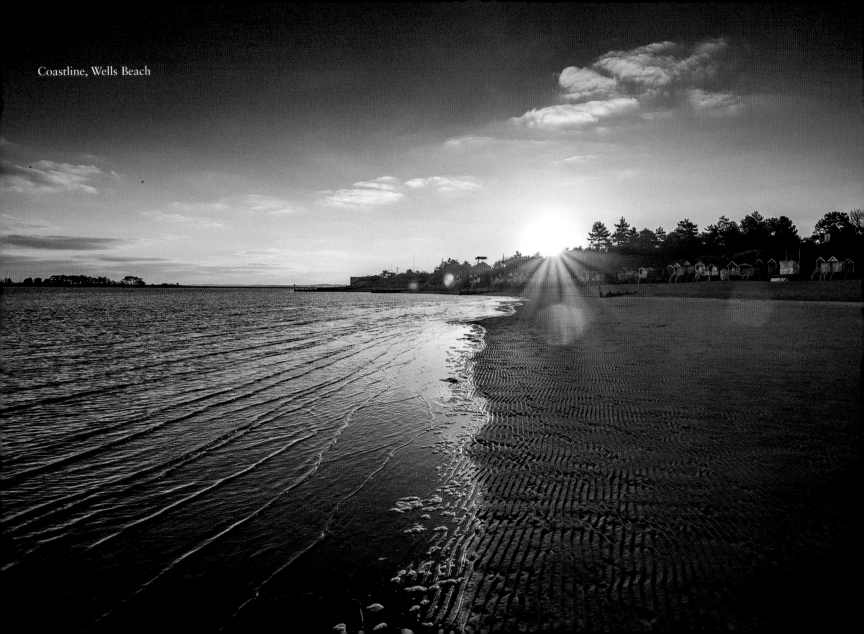

Coastline, Wells Beach

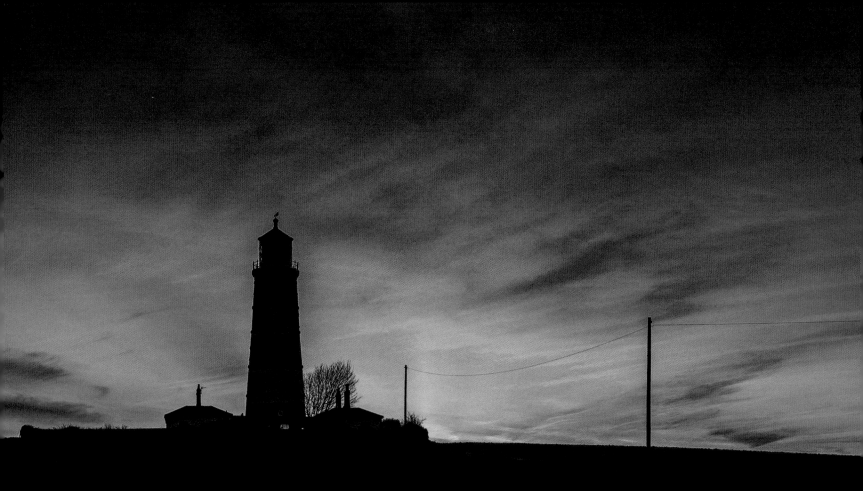

Colour of light, Happisburgh Lighthouse

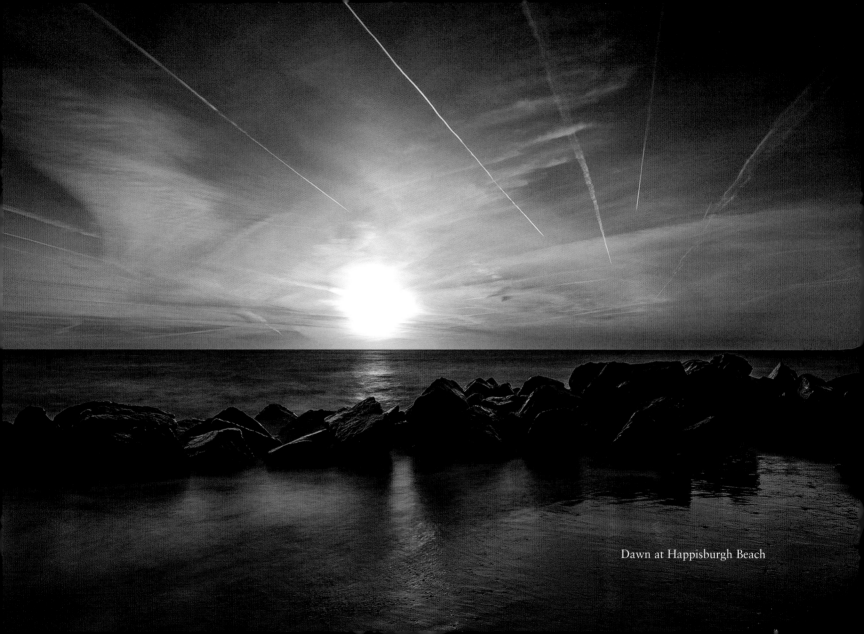

Dawn at Happisburgh Beach

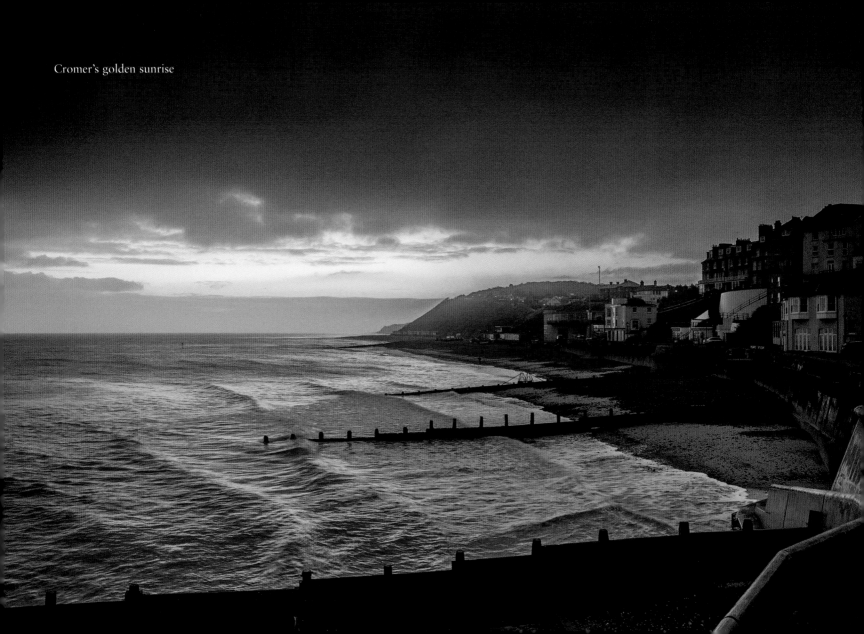

Cromer's golden sunrise

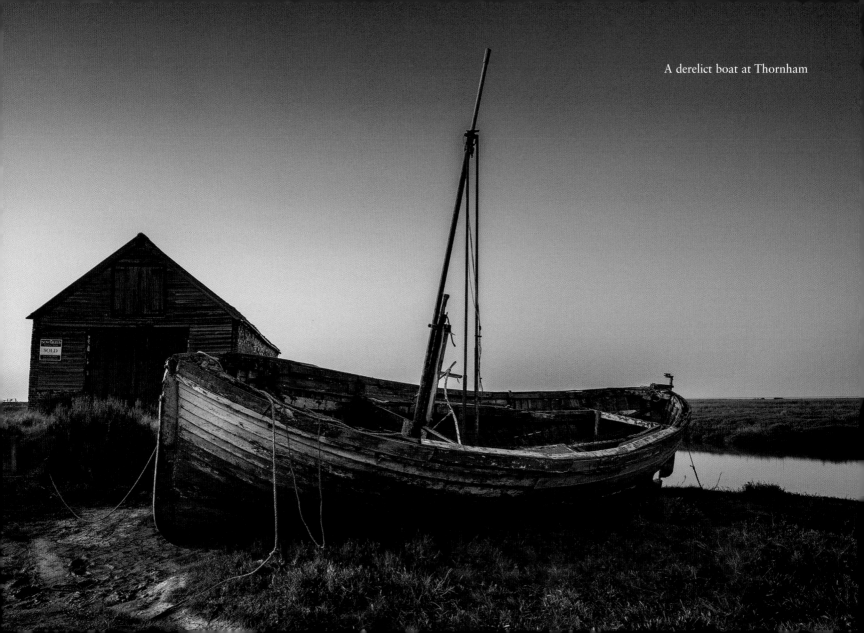

A derelict boat at Thornham

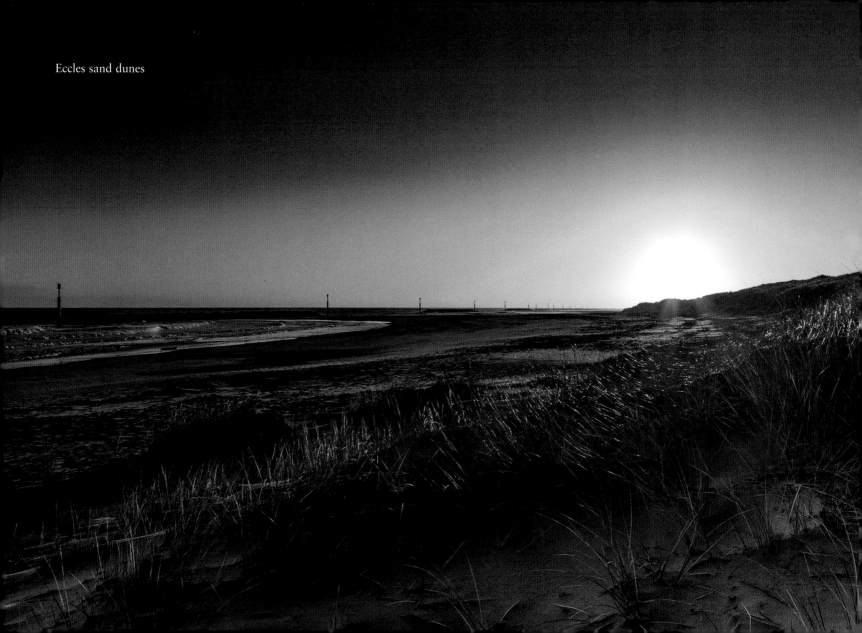

Eccles sand dunes

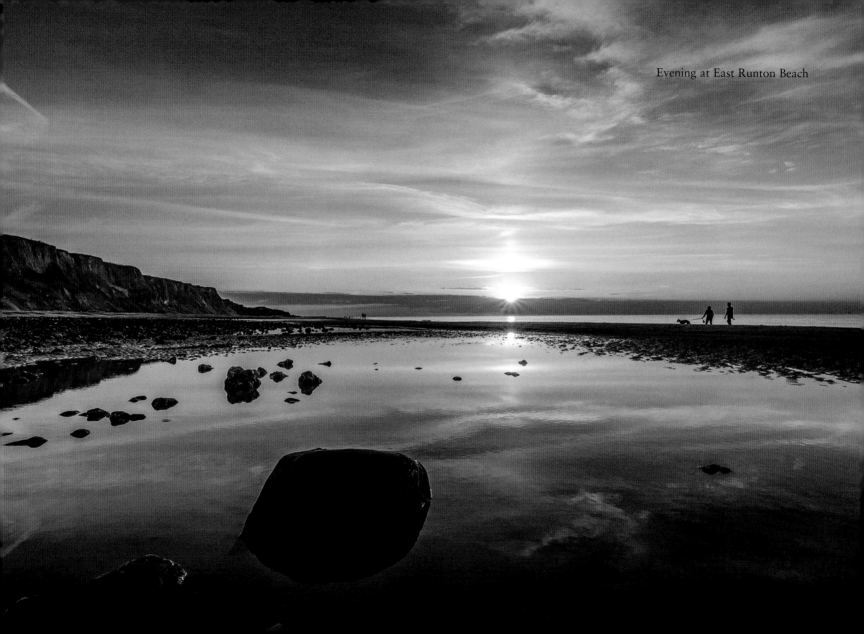

Evening at East Runton Beach

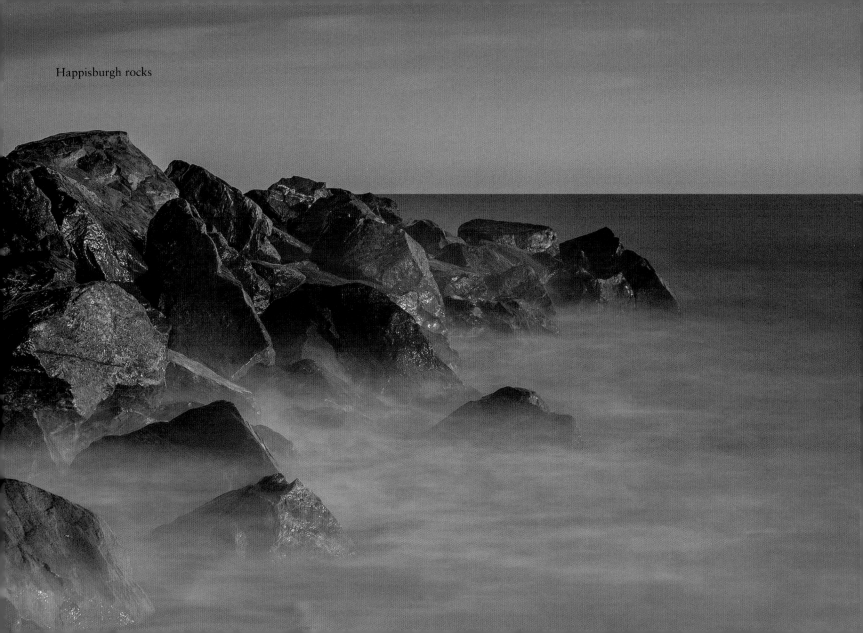

Happisburgh rocks

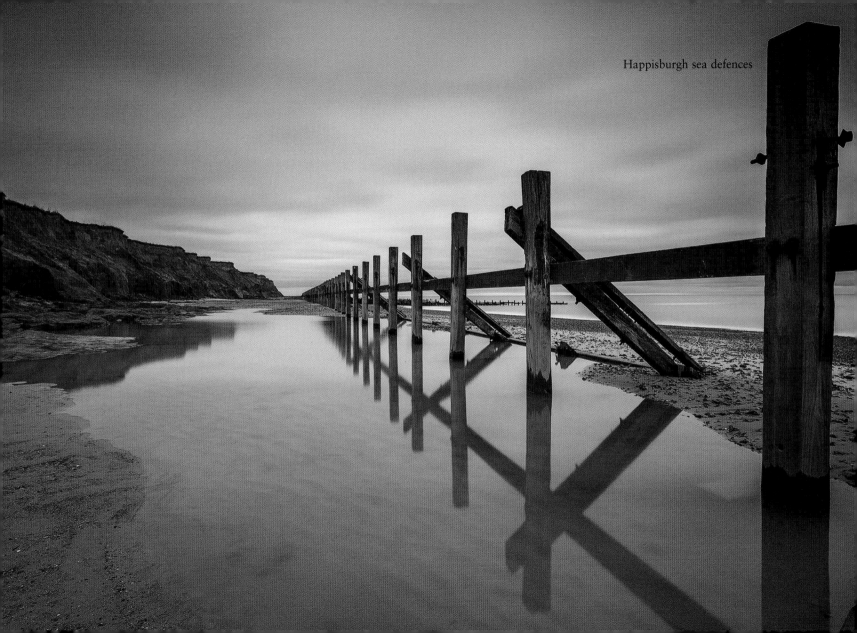

Happisburgh sea defences

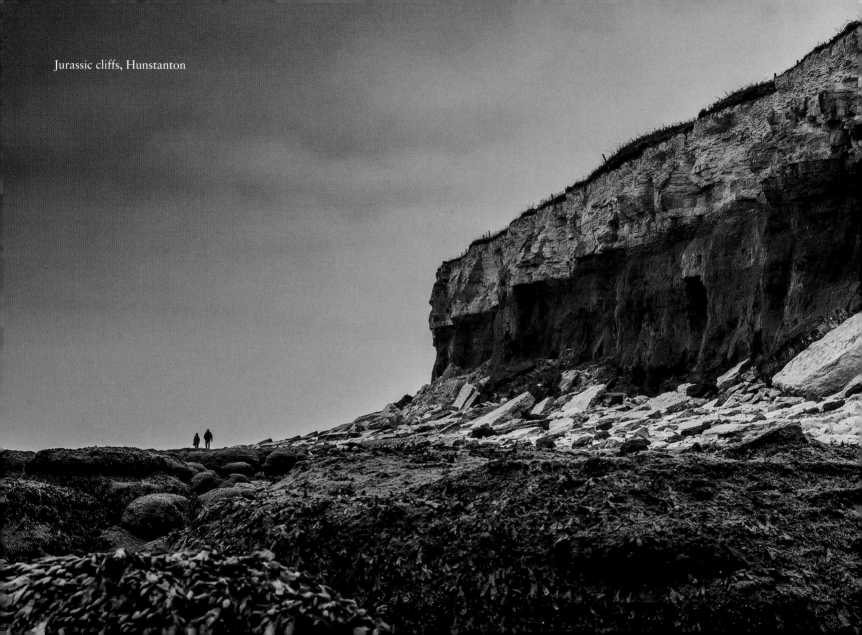

Jurassic cliffs, Hunstanton

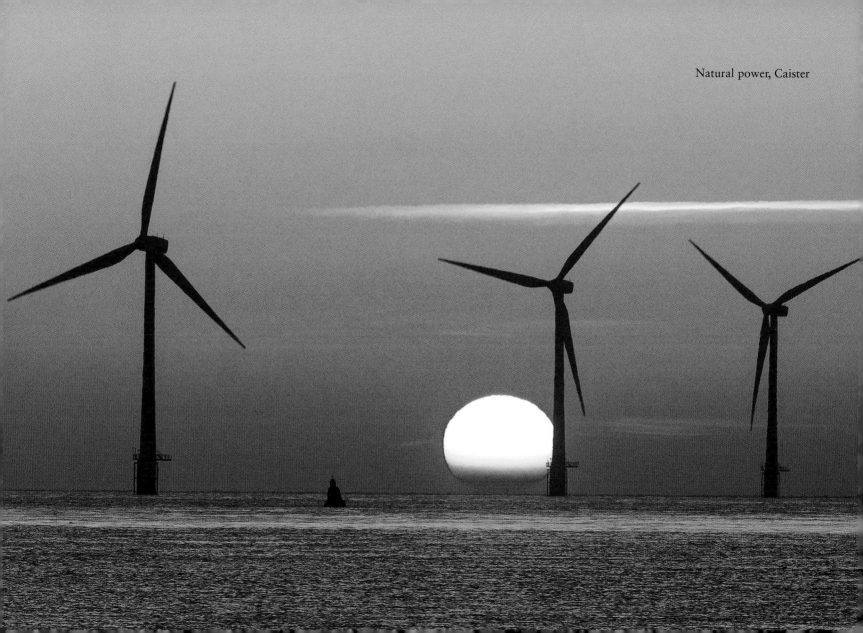

Natural power, Caister

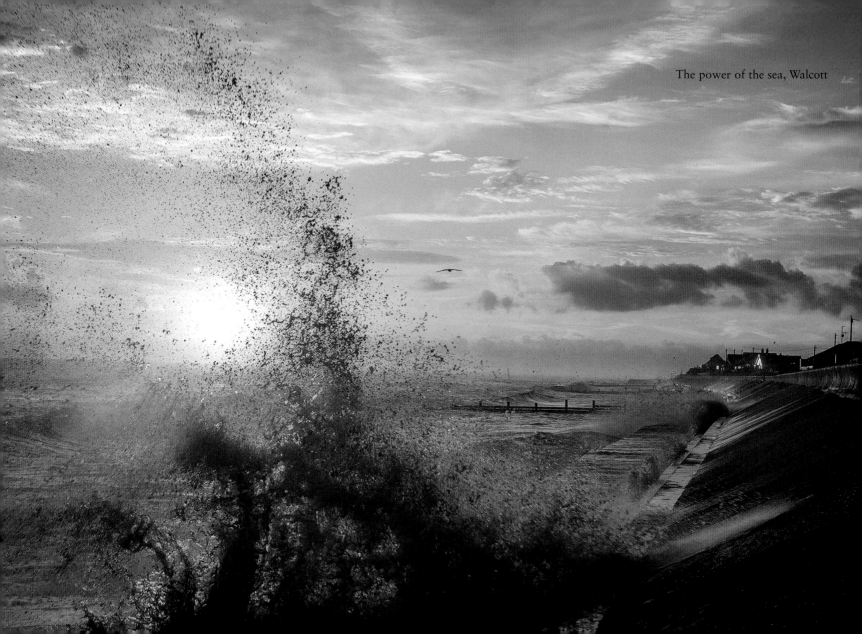

The power of the sea, Walcott

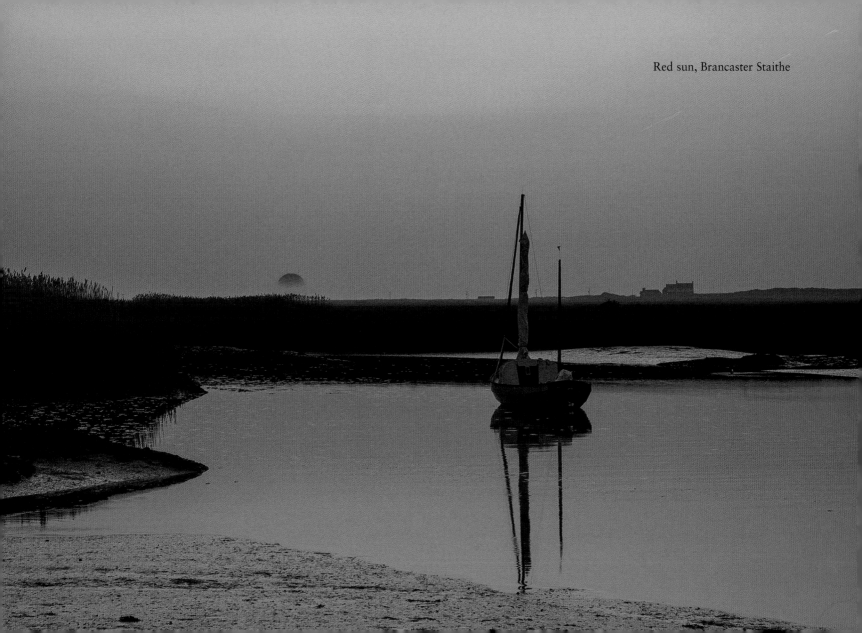

Red sun, Brancaster Staithe

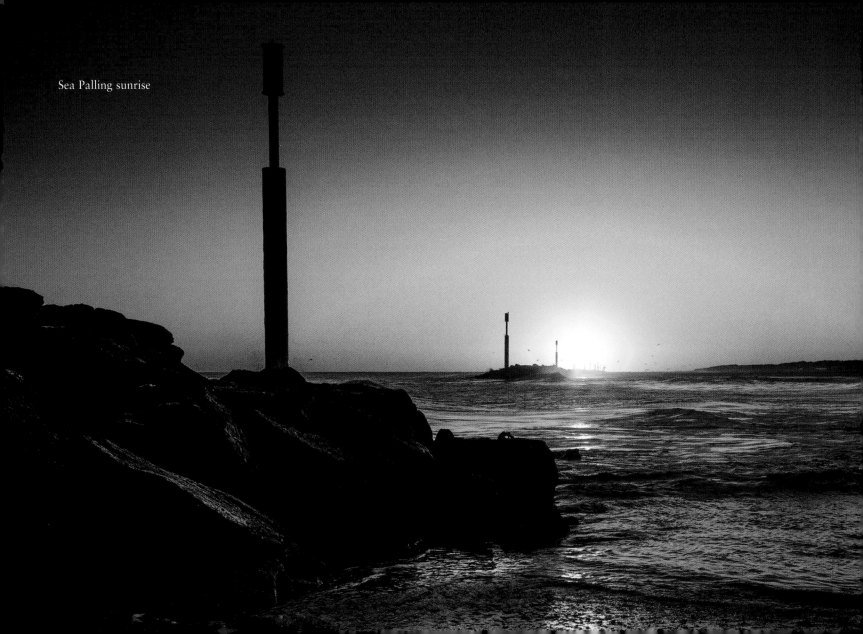

Sea Palling sunrise

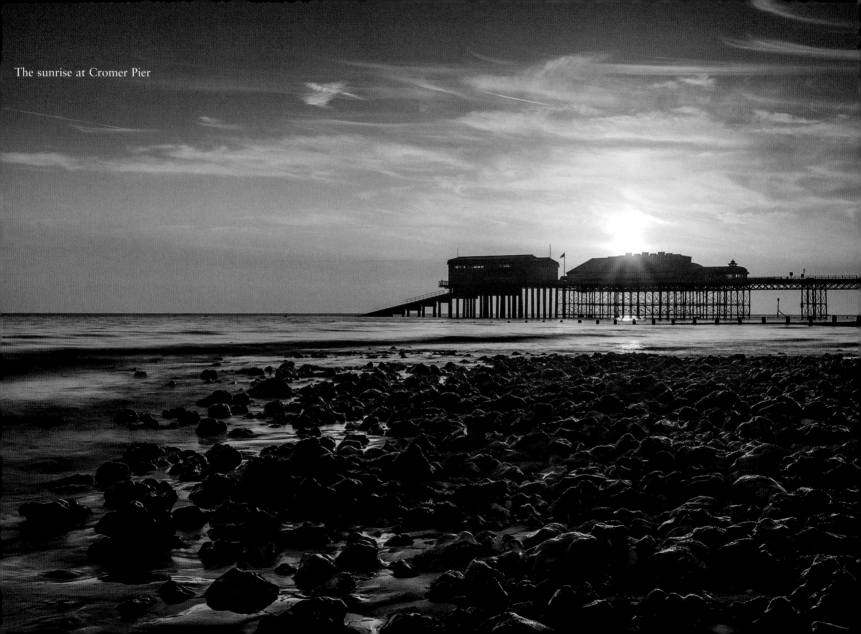

The sunrise at Cromer Pier

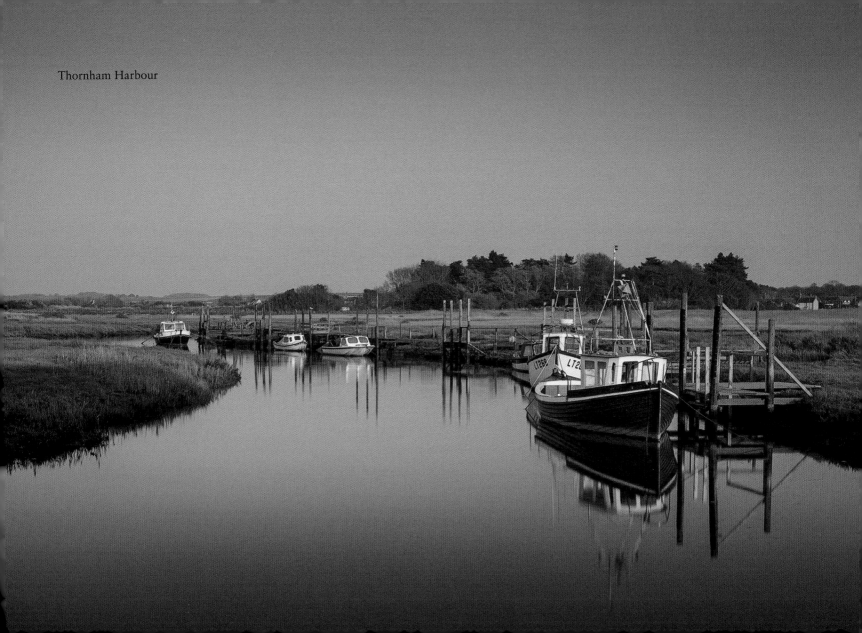

Thornham Harbour

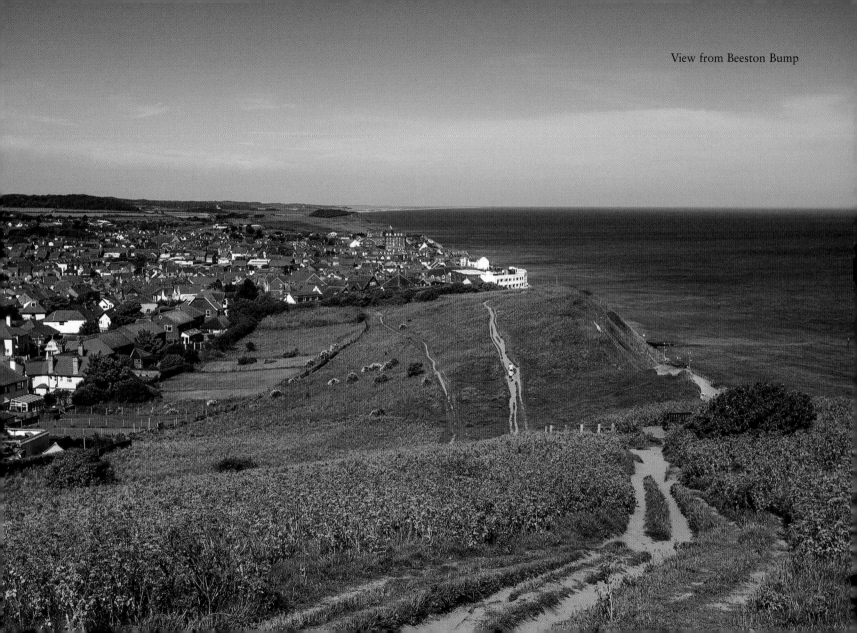

View from Beeston Bump

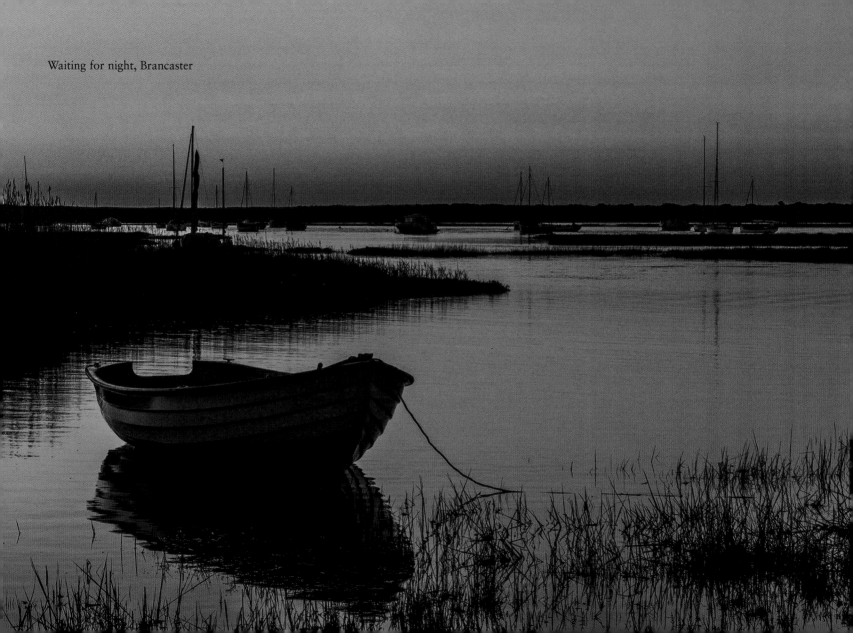

Waiting for night, Brancaster

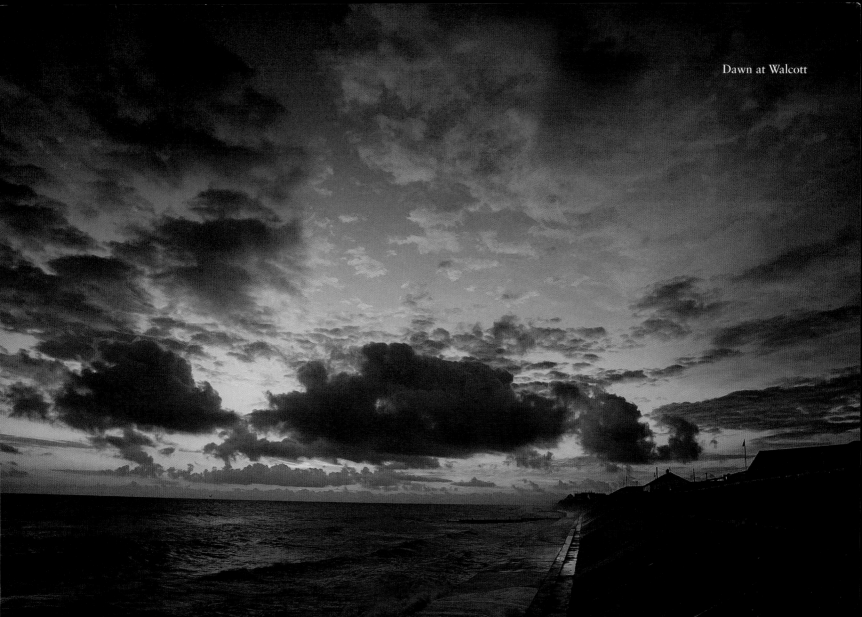

Dawn at Walcott

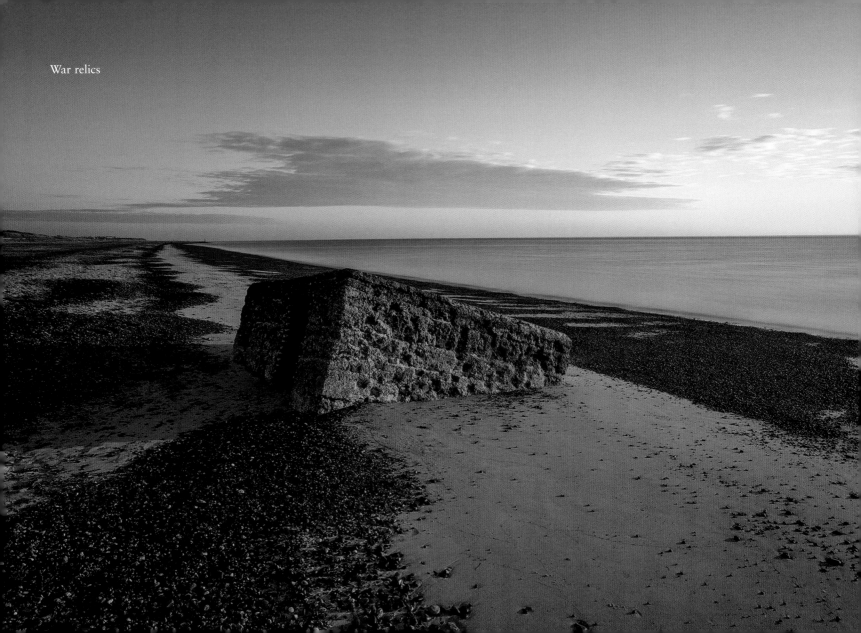

War relics

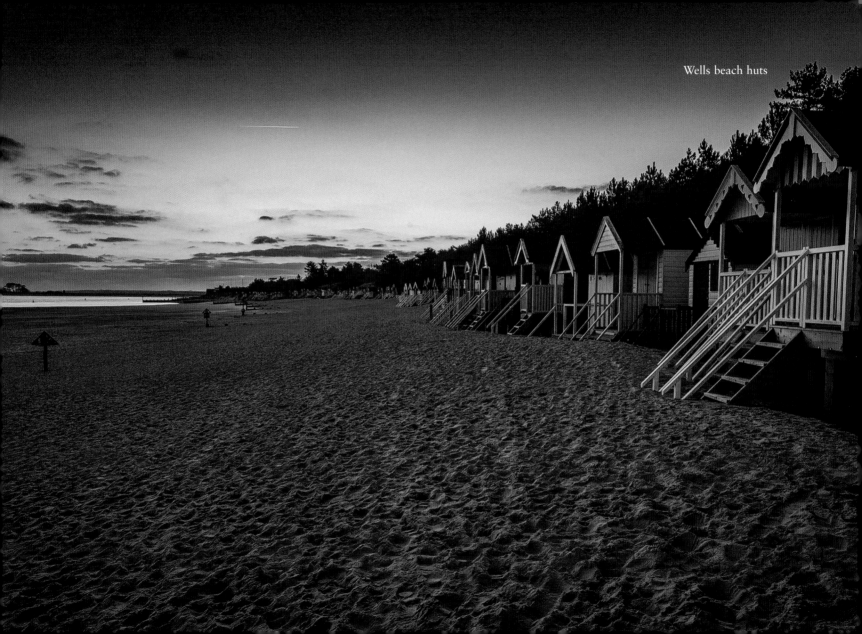

Wells beach huts

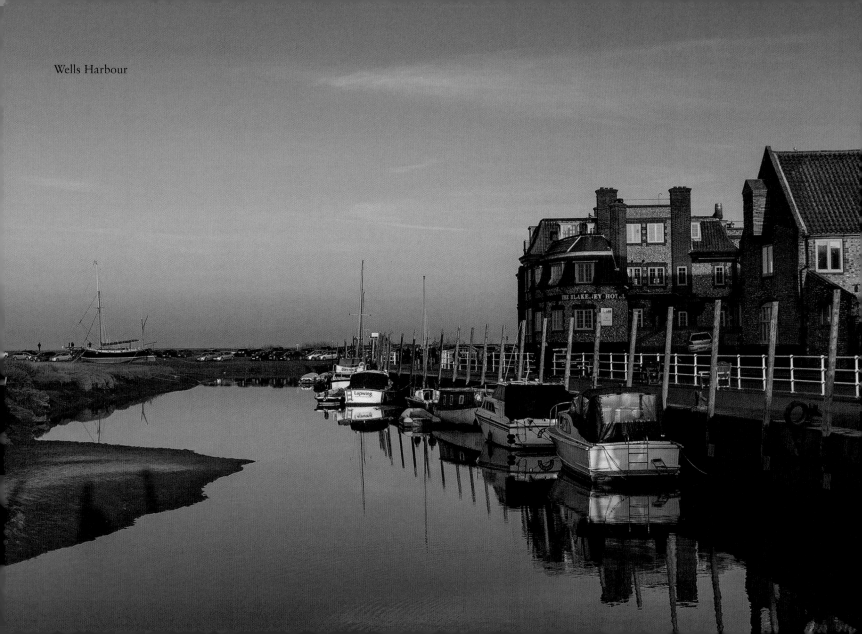

Wells Harbour

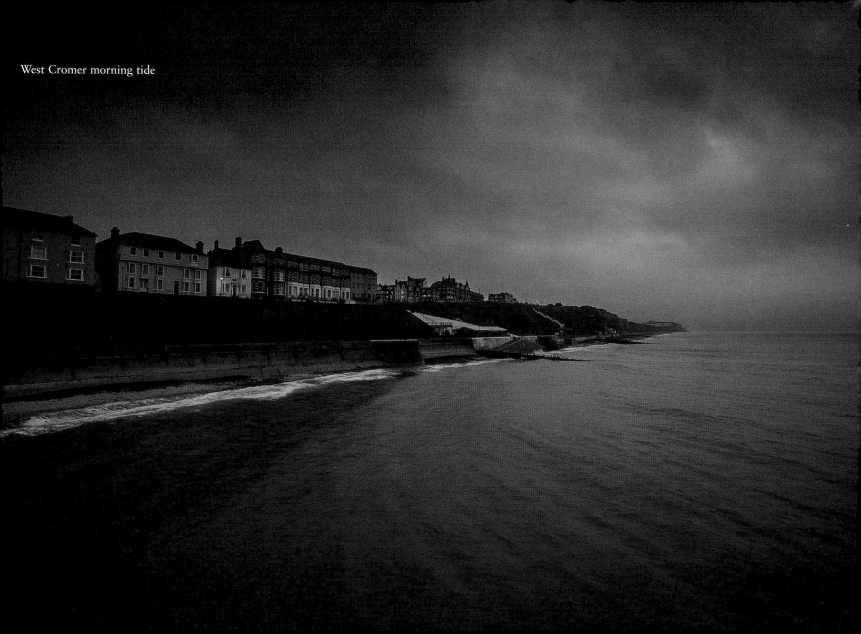

West Cromer morning tide

# NIGHT-TIME NORFOLK

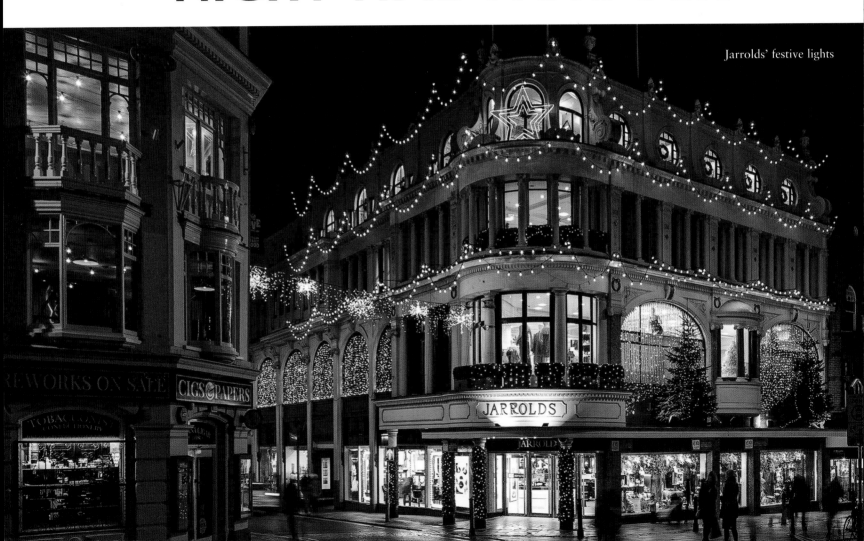

Jarrolds' festive lights

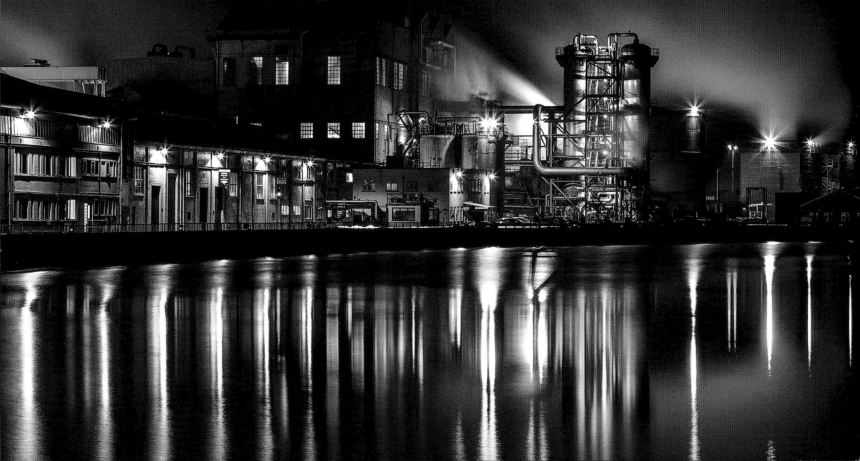

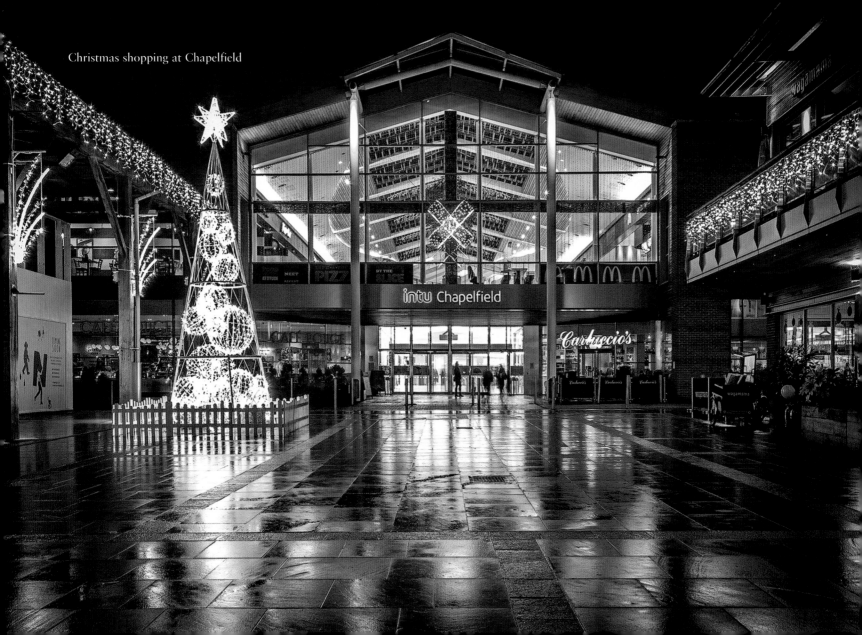

Christmas shopping at Chapelfield

A festive Blickling Hall

Moonrise at Turf Fen

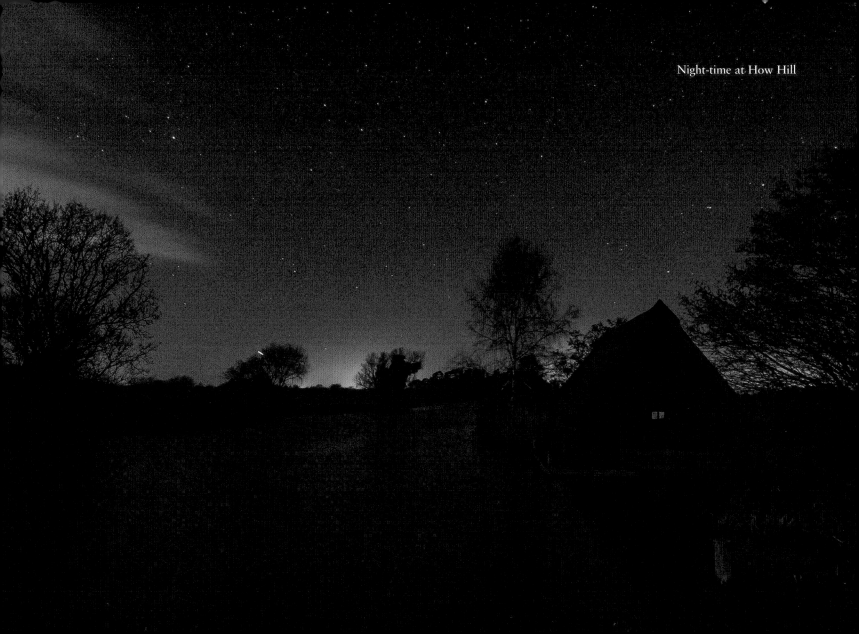

Night-time at How Hill

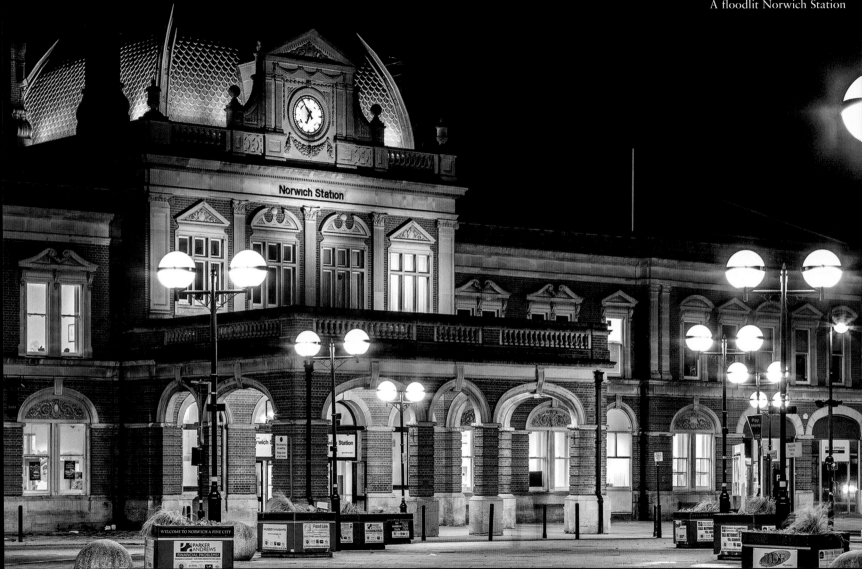

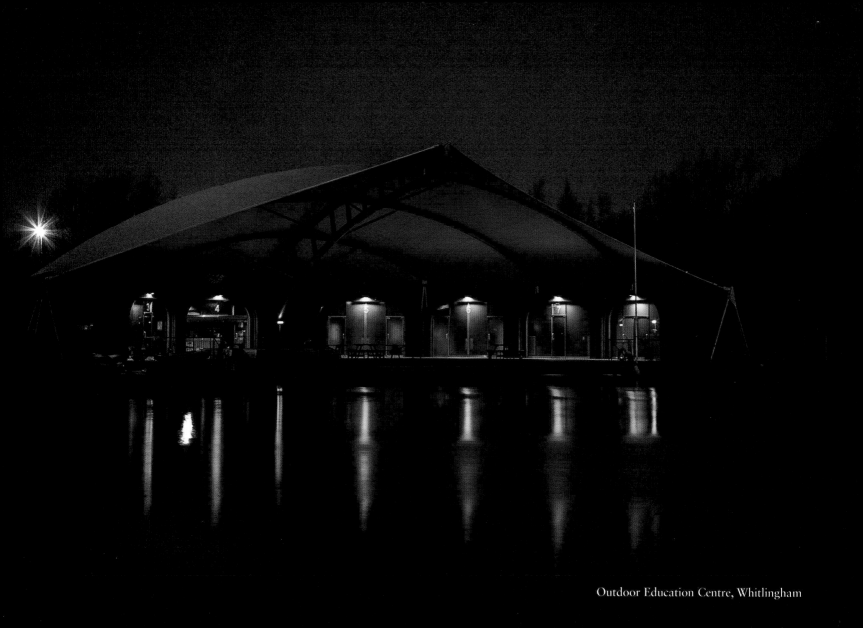

Outdoor Education Centre, Whitlingham

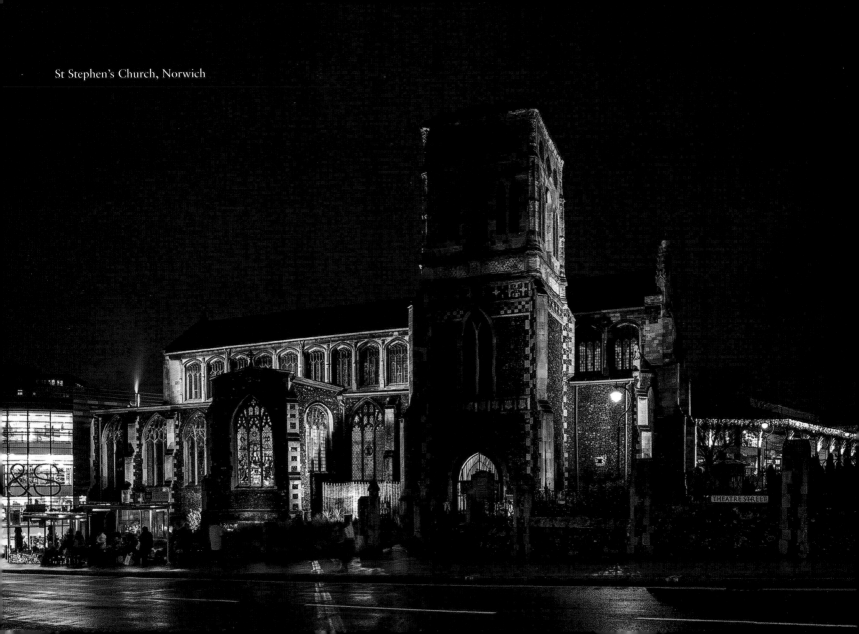

St Stephen's Church, Norwich

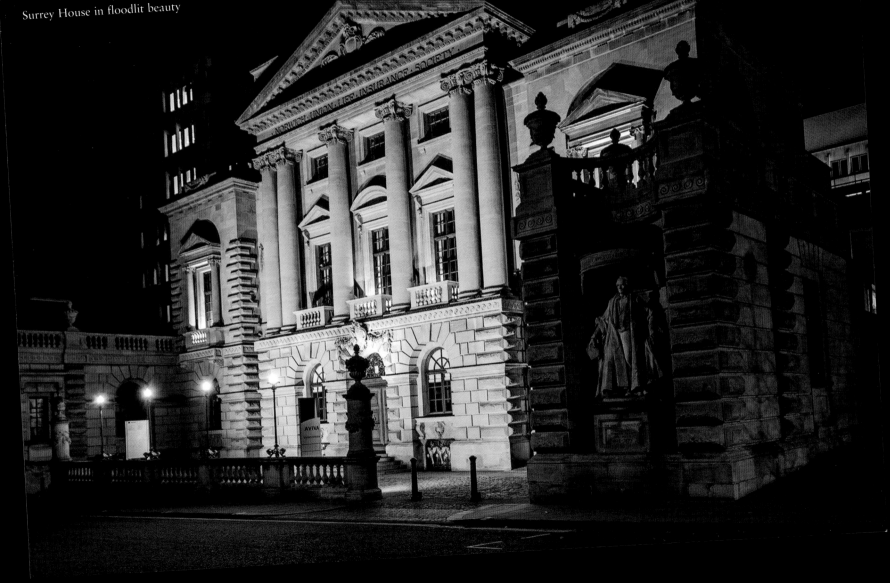
Surrey House in floodlit beauty

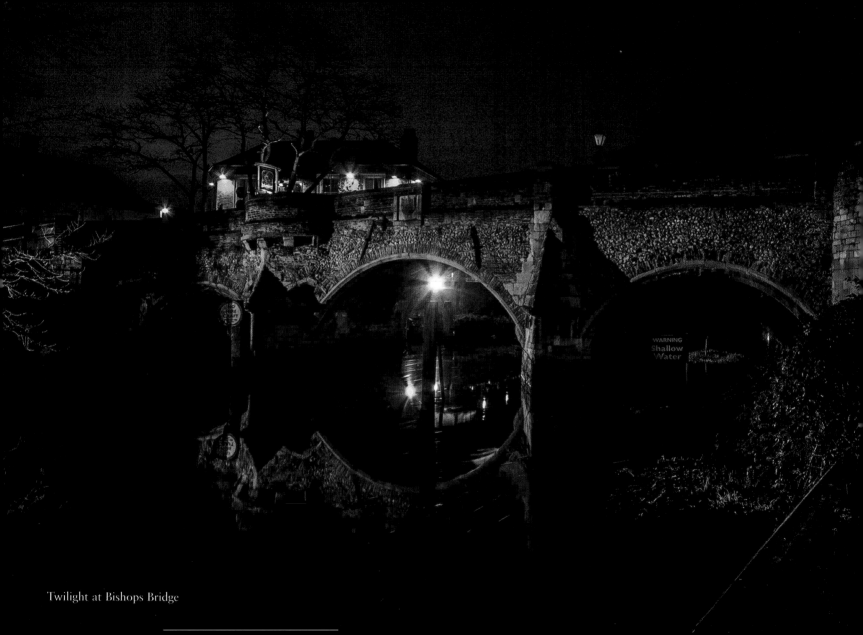

Twilight at Bishops Bridge

WARNING
Shallow
Water

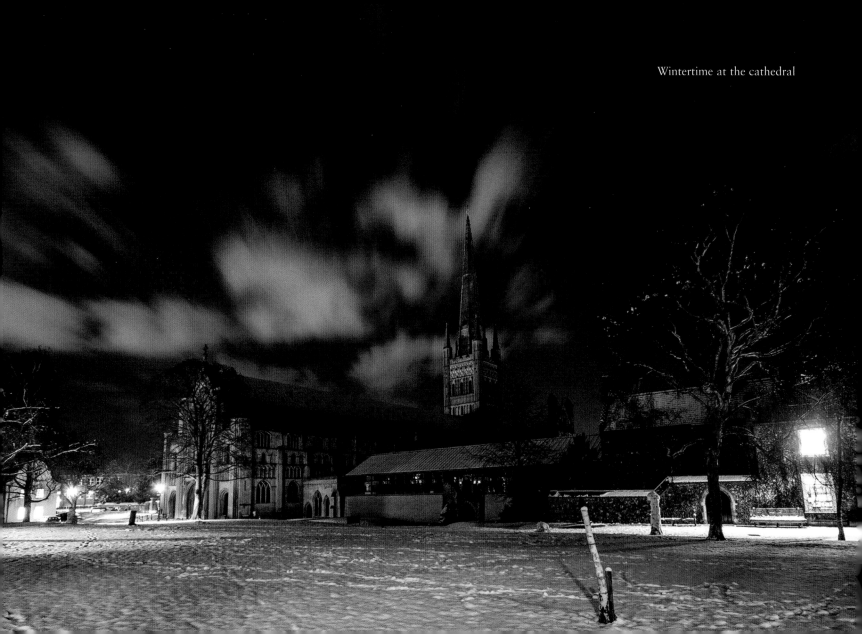

Wintertime at the cathedral

# NORWICH

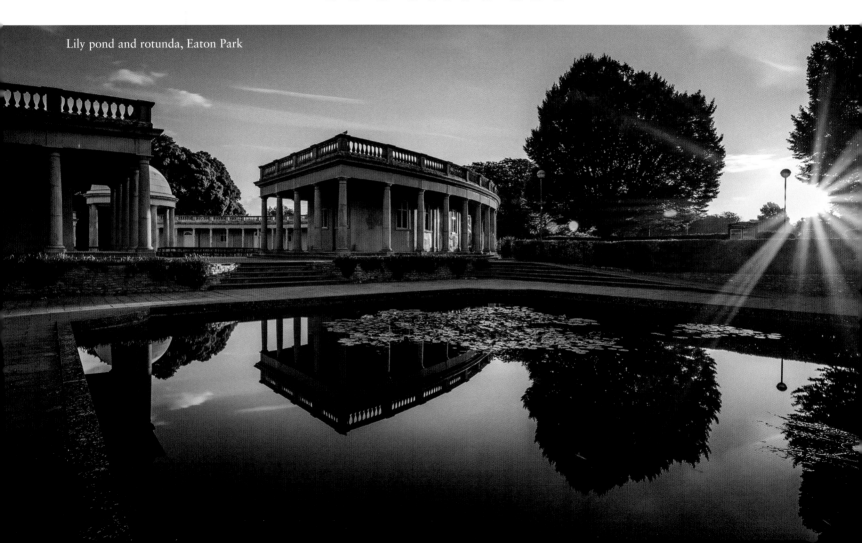

Lily pond and rotunda, Eaton Park

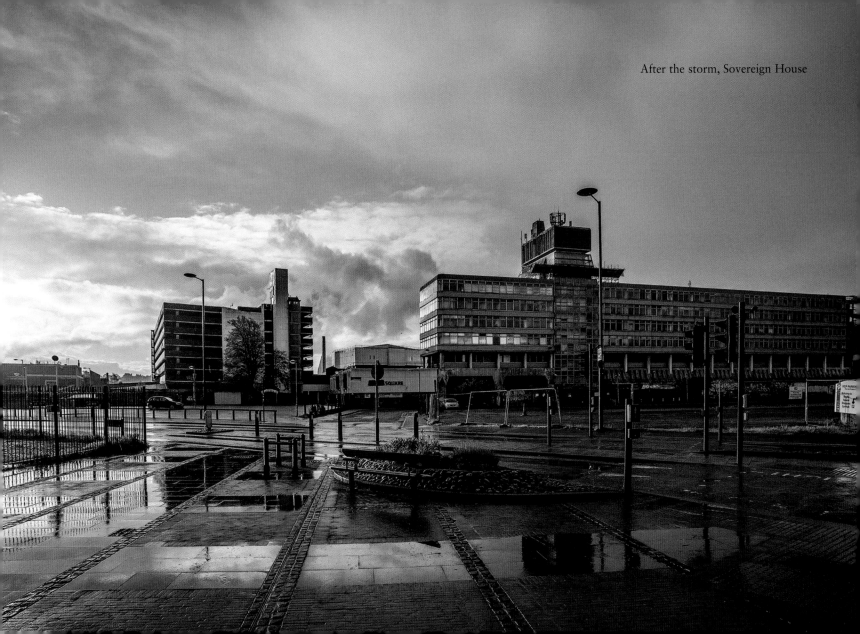

After the storm, Sovereign House

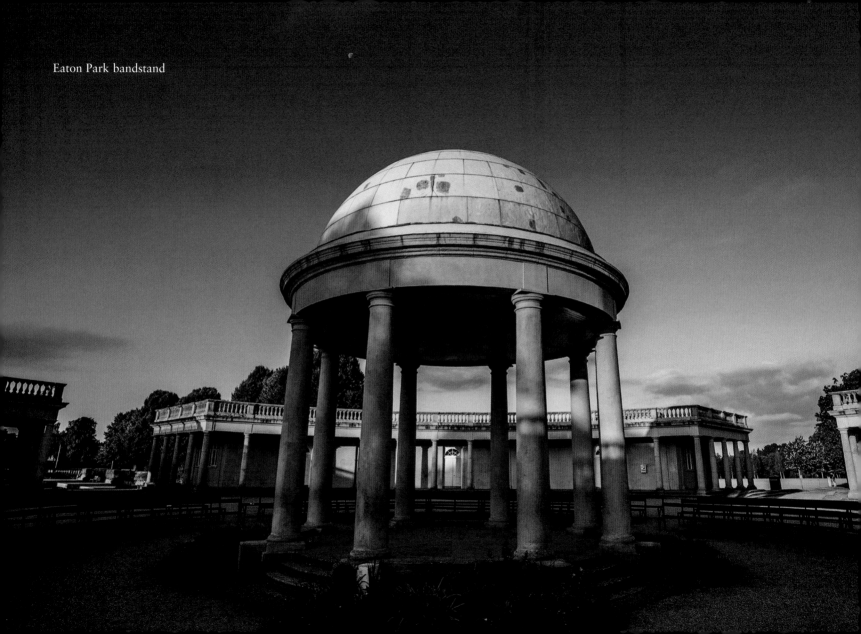

Eaton Park bandstand

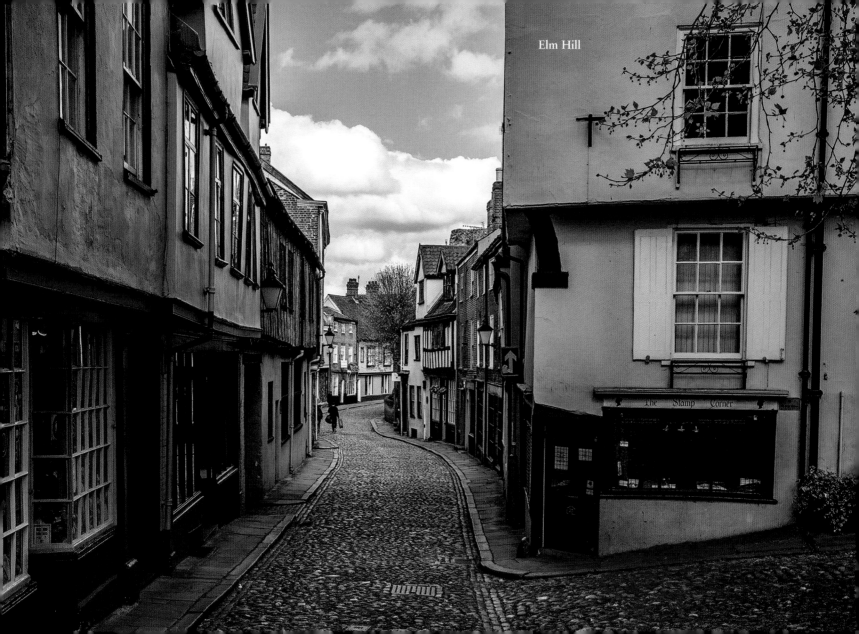

Elm Hill

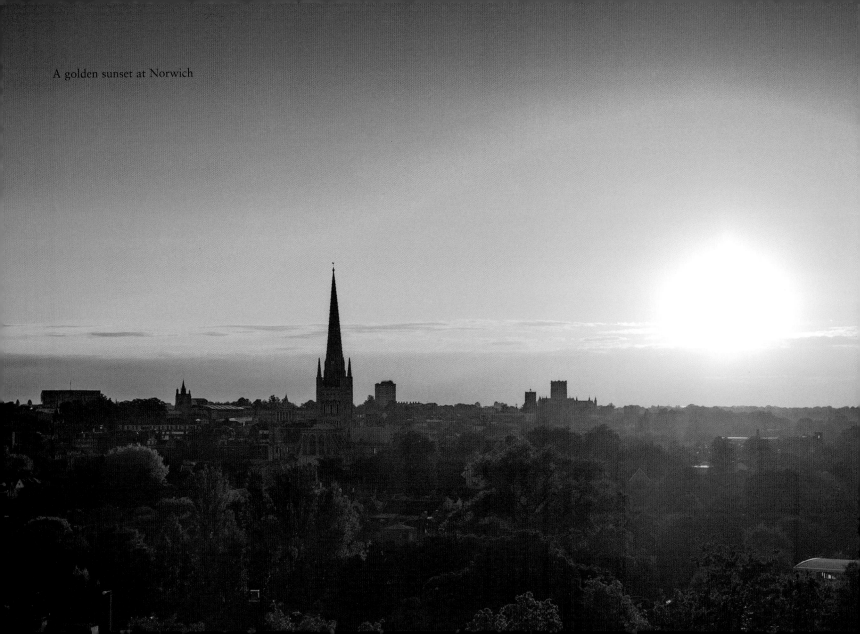

A golden sunset at Norwich

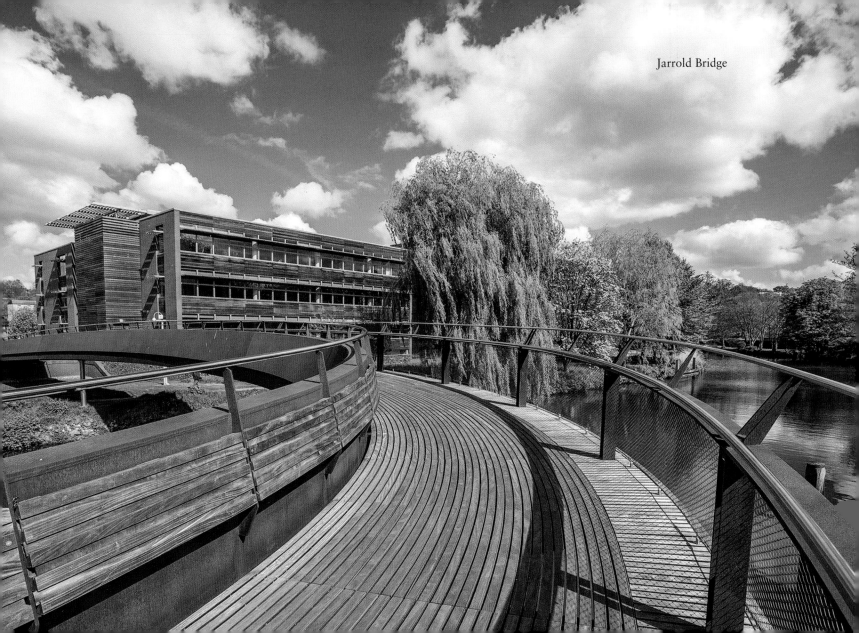

Jarrold Bridge

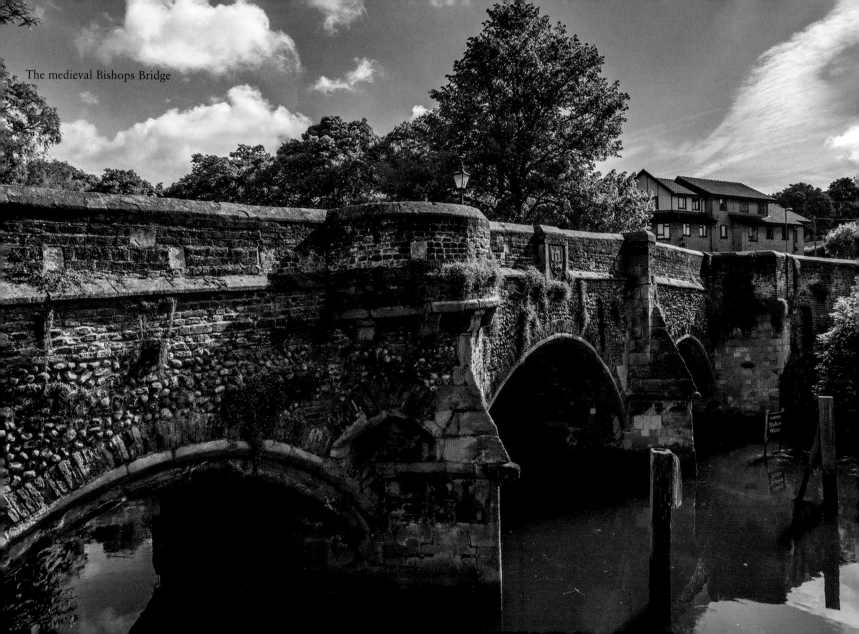

The medieval Bishops Bridge

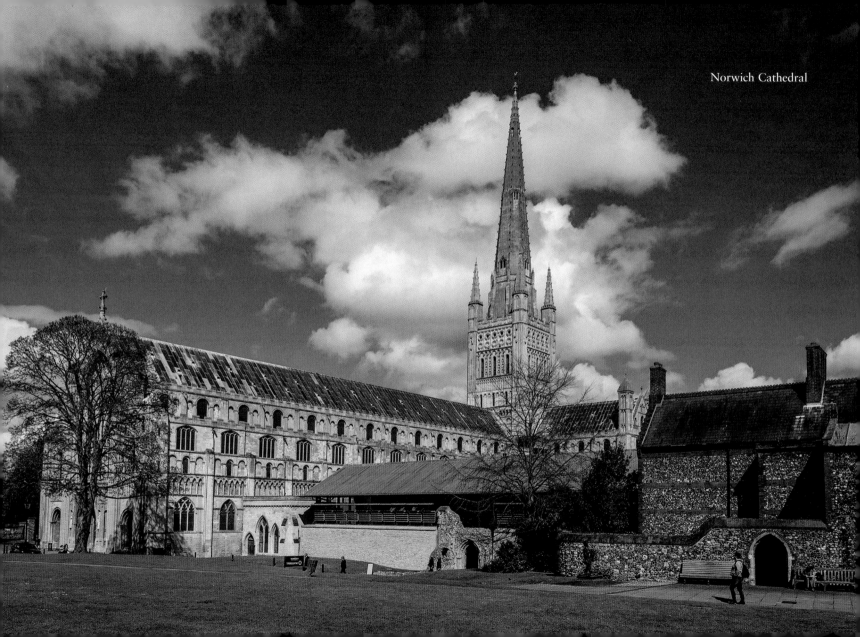
Norwich Cathedral

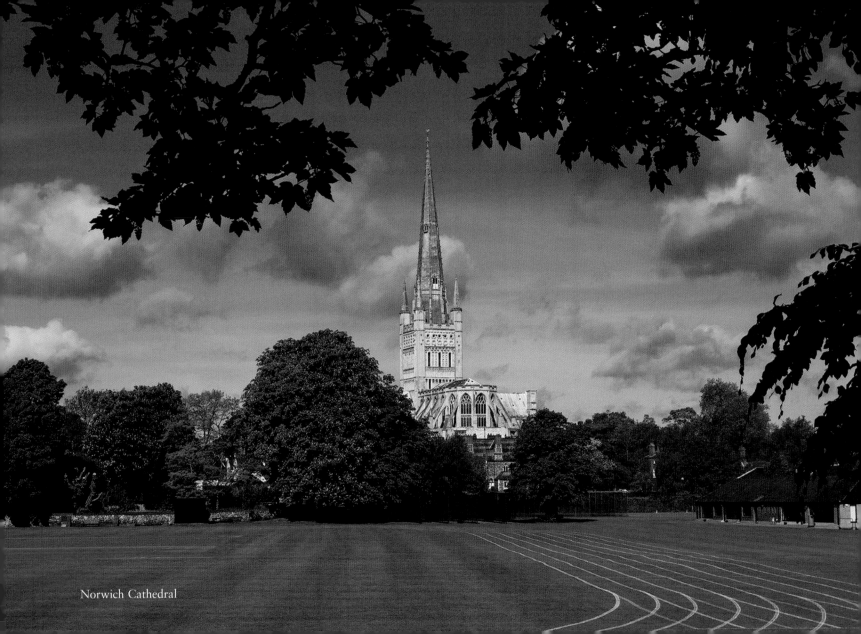

Norwich Cathedral

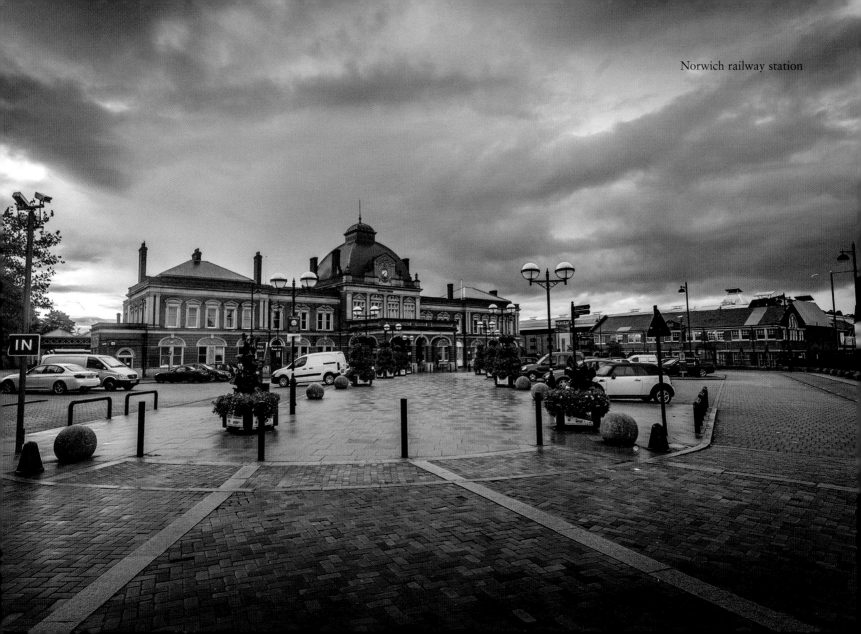

Norwich railway station

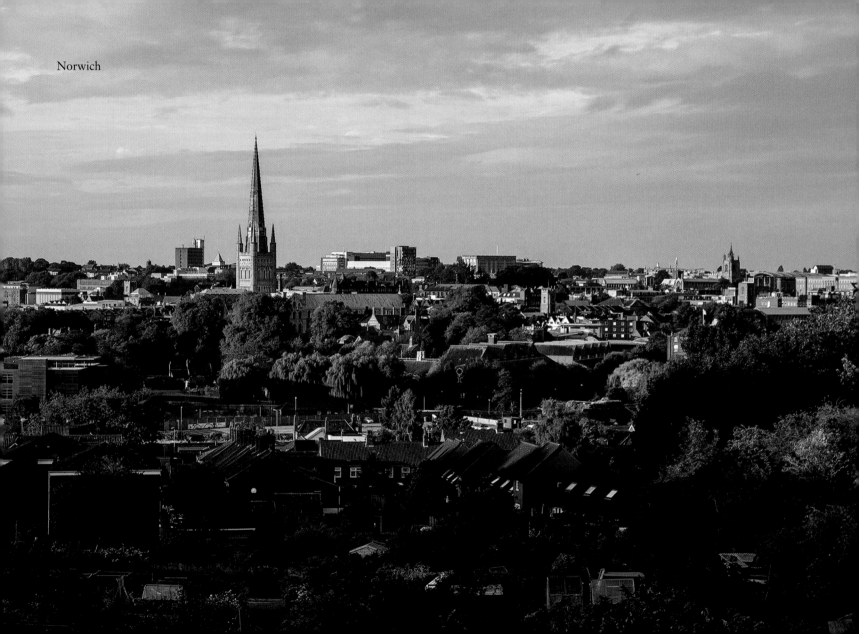

Norwich

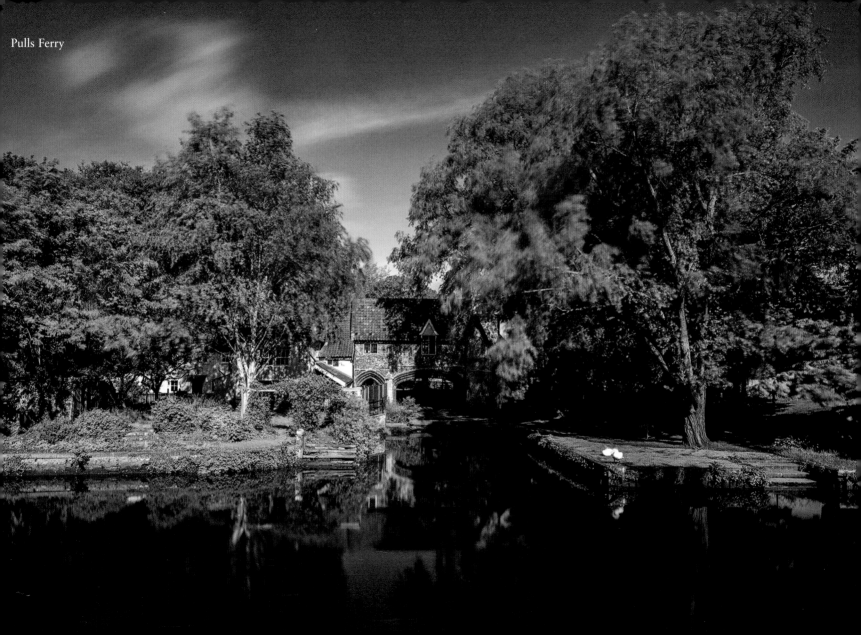

Pulls Ferry

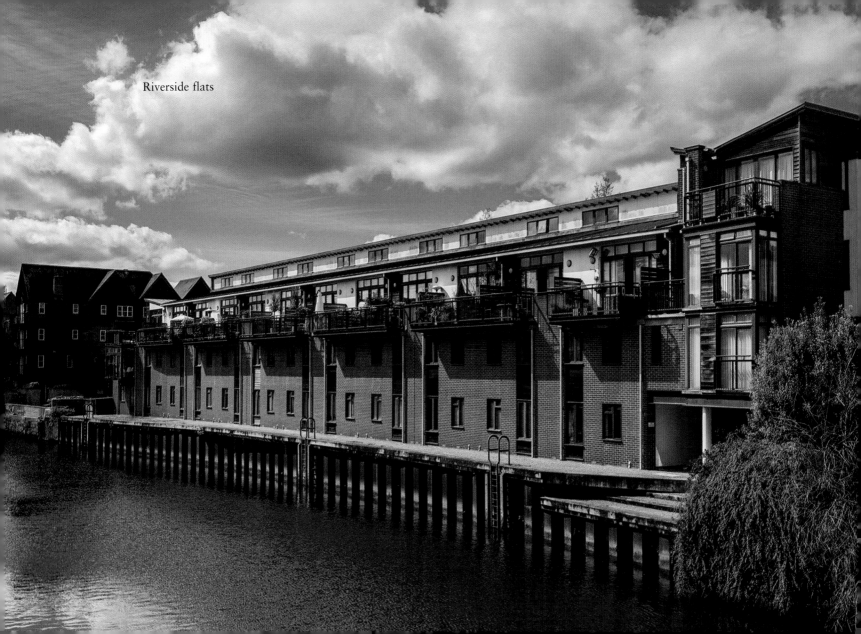

Riverside flats

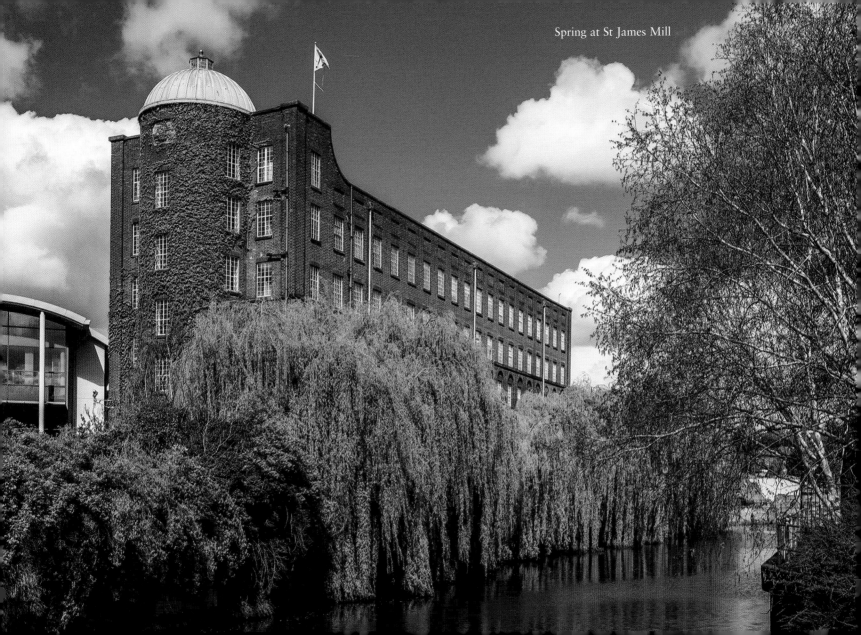
Spring at St James Mill

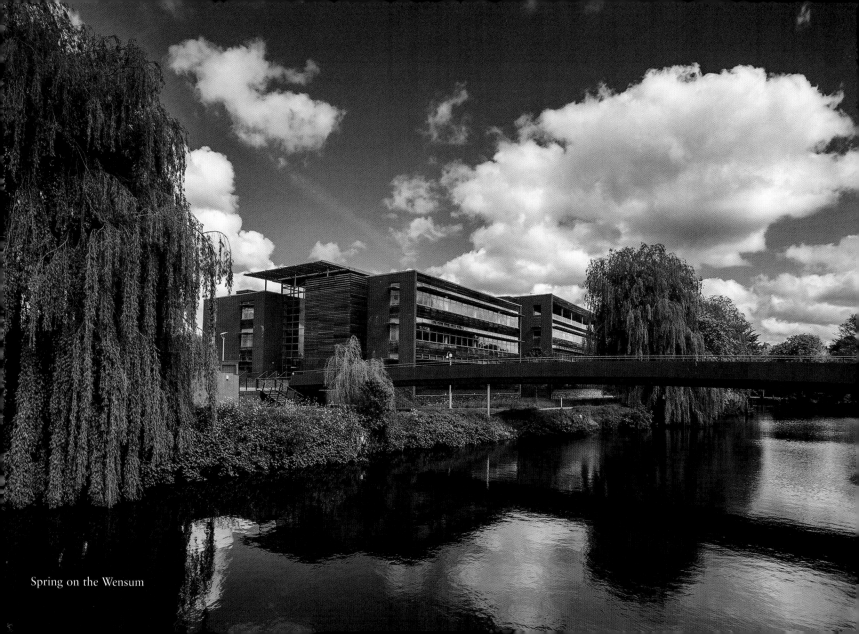

Spring on the Wensum

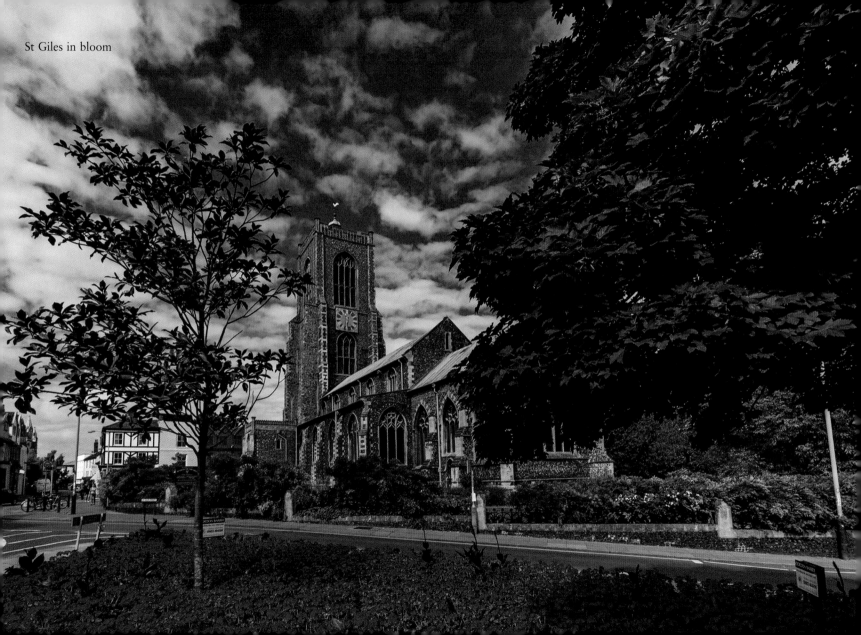

St Giles in bloom

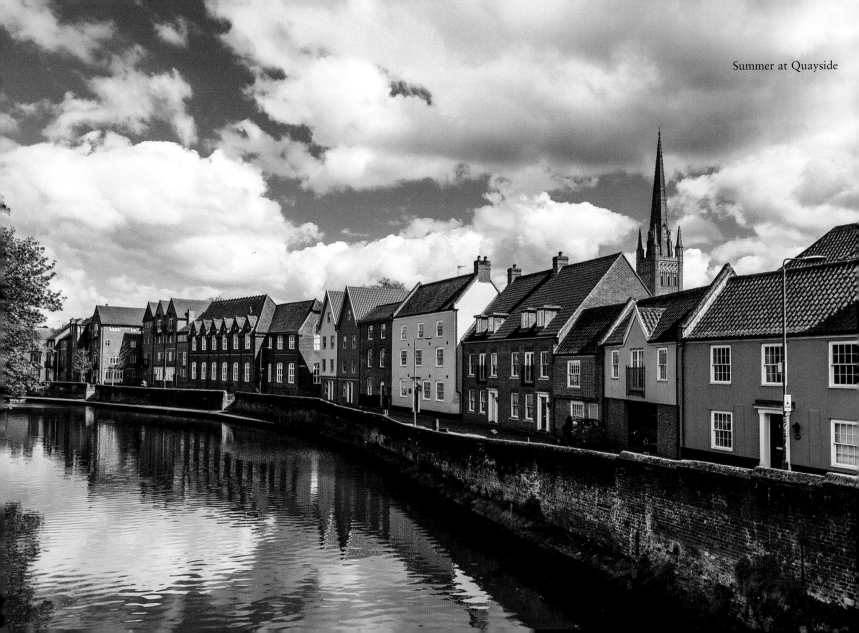

Summer at Quayside

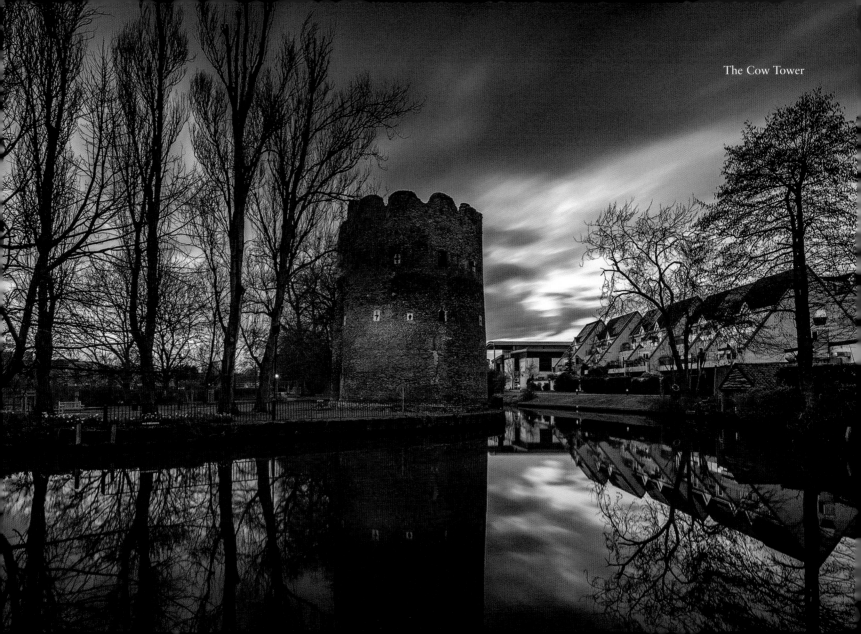
The Cow Tower

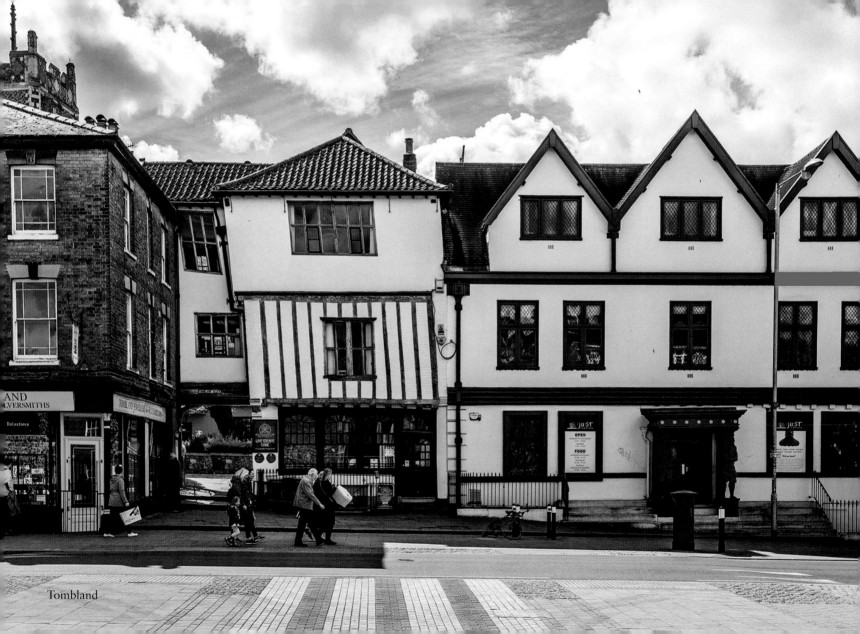

Tombland

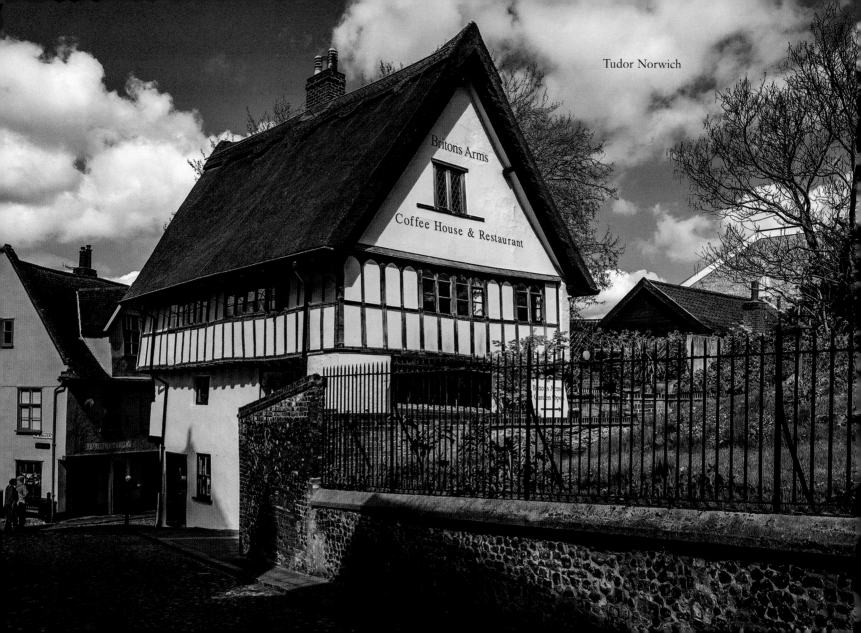

Tudor Norwich

Britons Arms

Coffee House & Restaurant

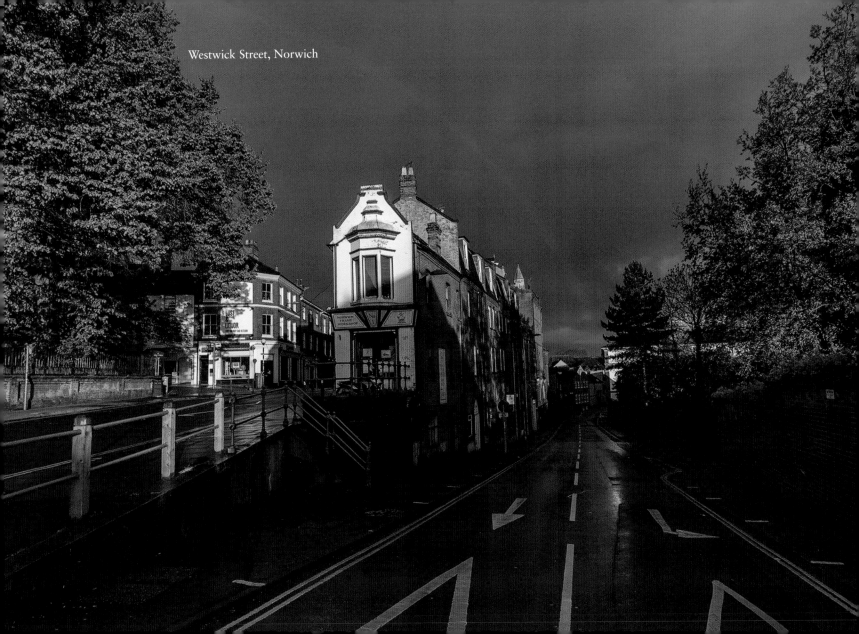

Westwick Street, Norwich

# THE NORFOLK BROADS

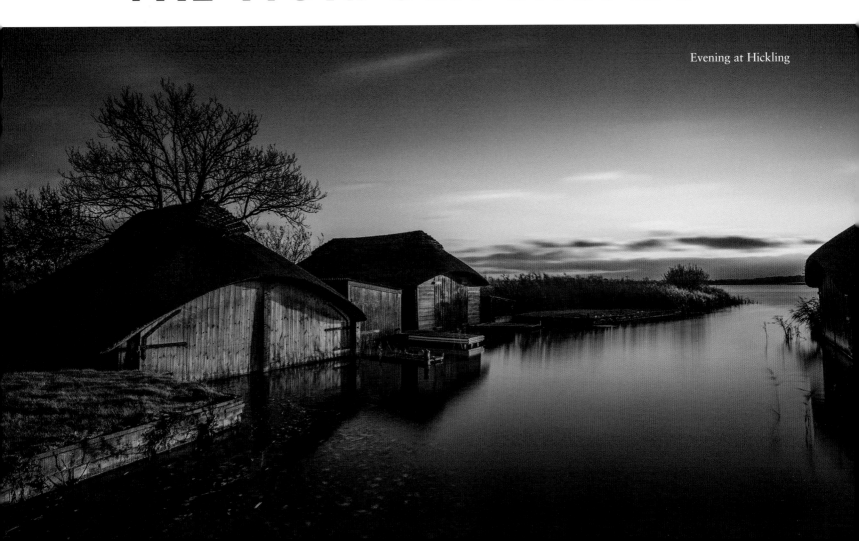

Evening at Hickling

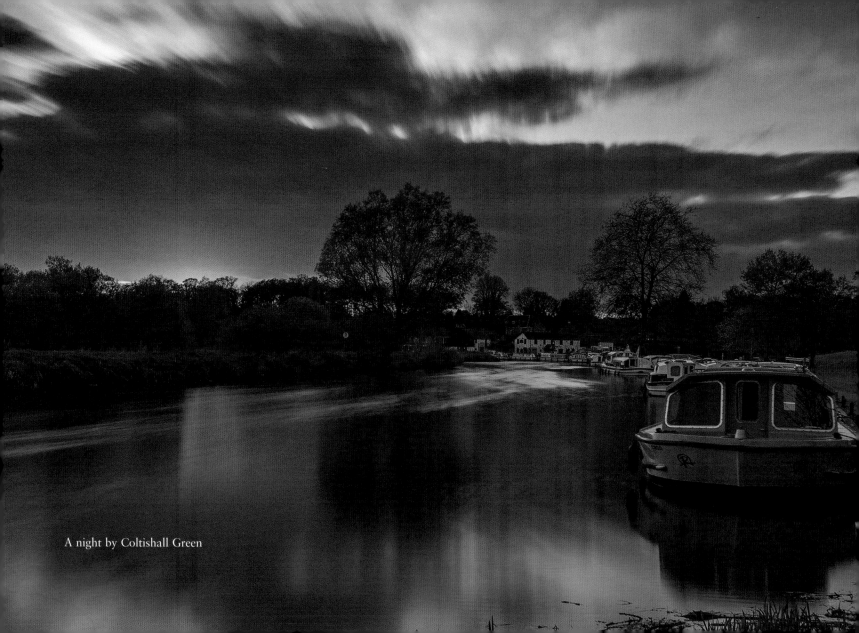

A night by Coltishall Green

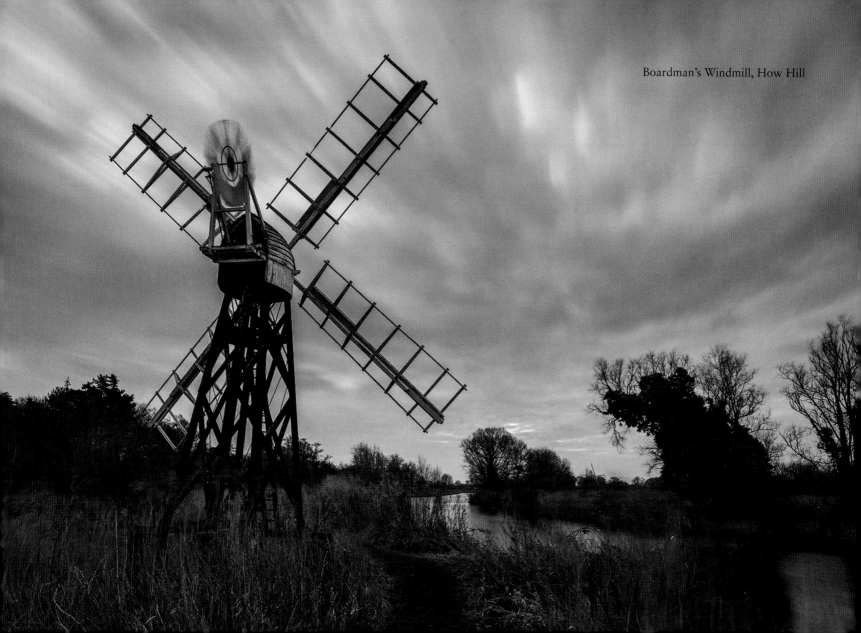

Boardman's Windmill, How Hill

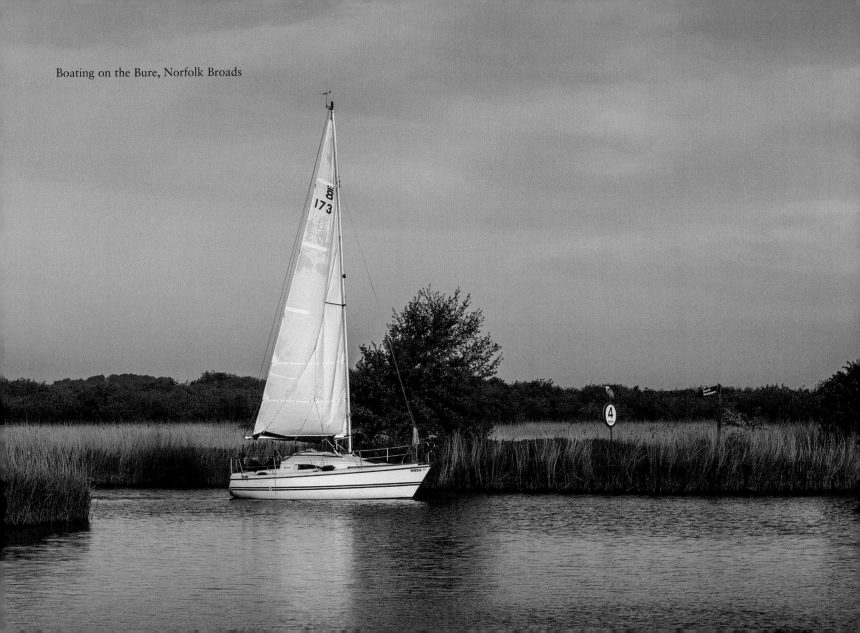

Boating on the Bure, Norfolk Broads

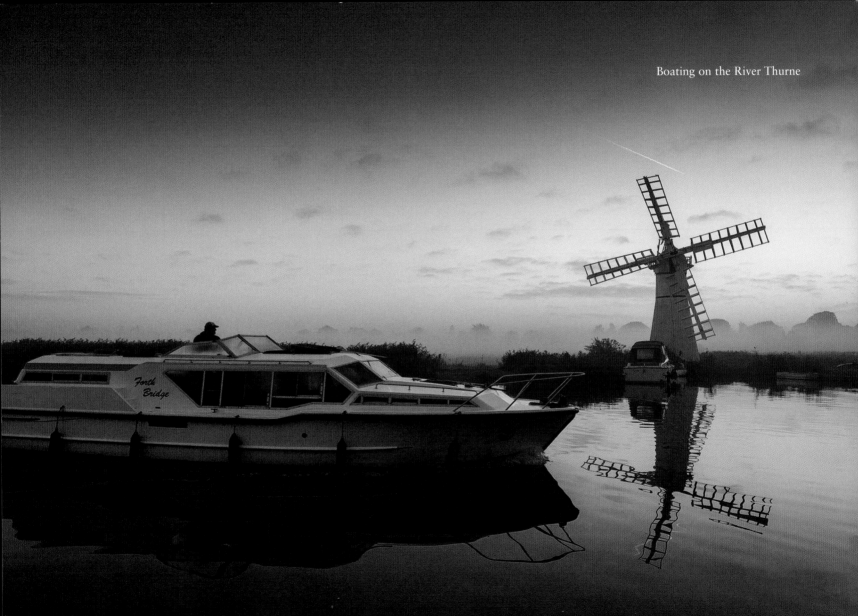

Boating on the River Thurne

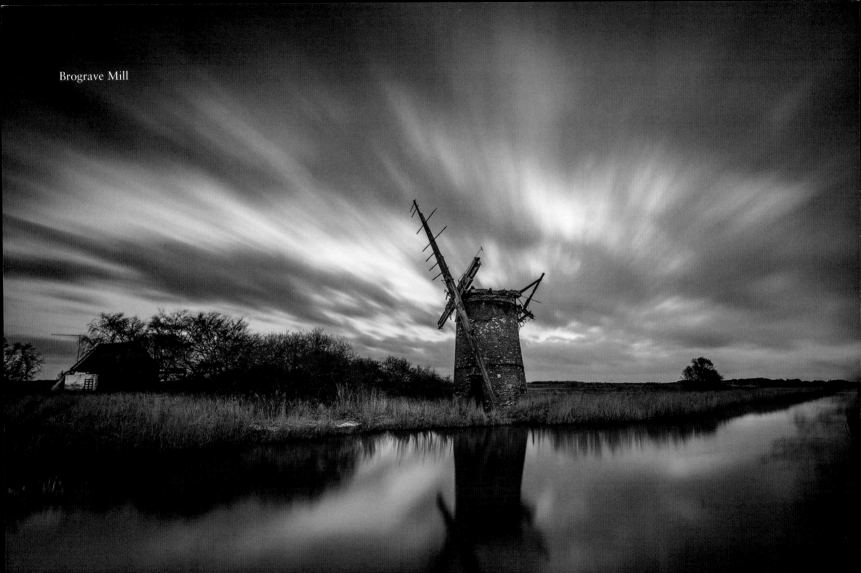

Brograve Mill

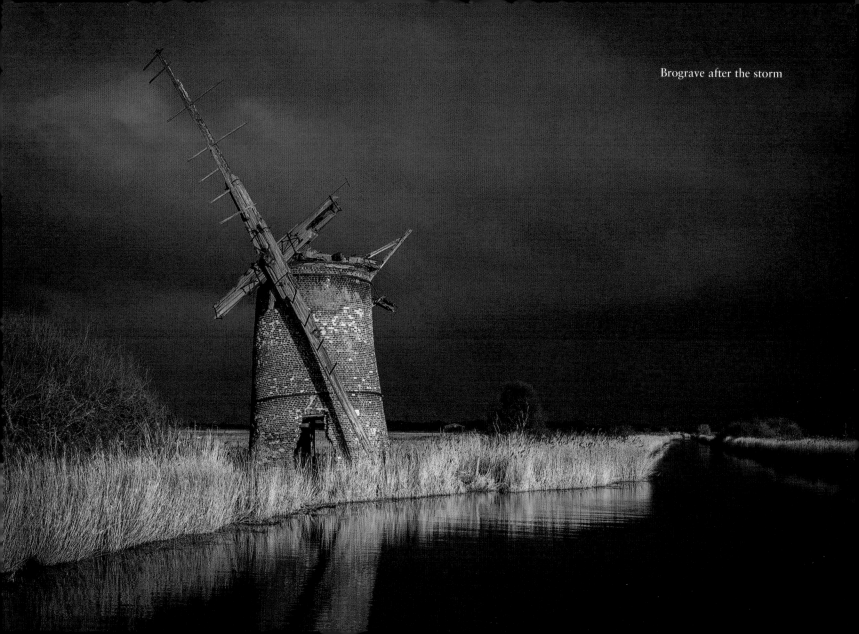

Brograve after the storm

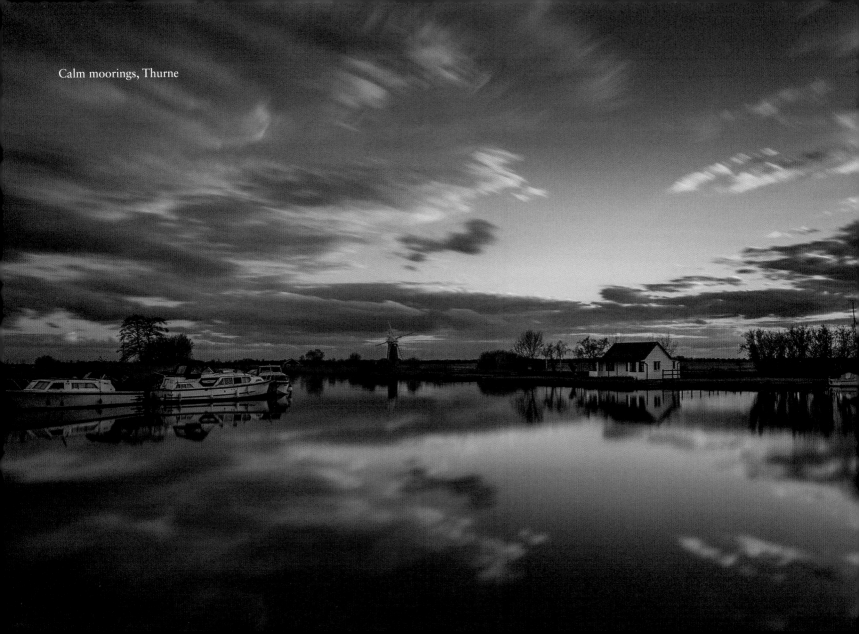

Calm moorings, Thurne

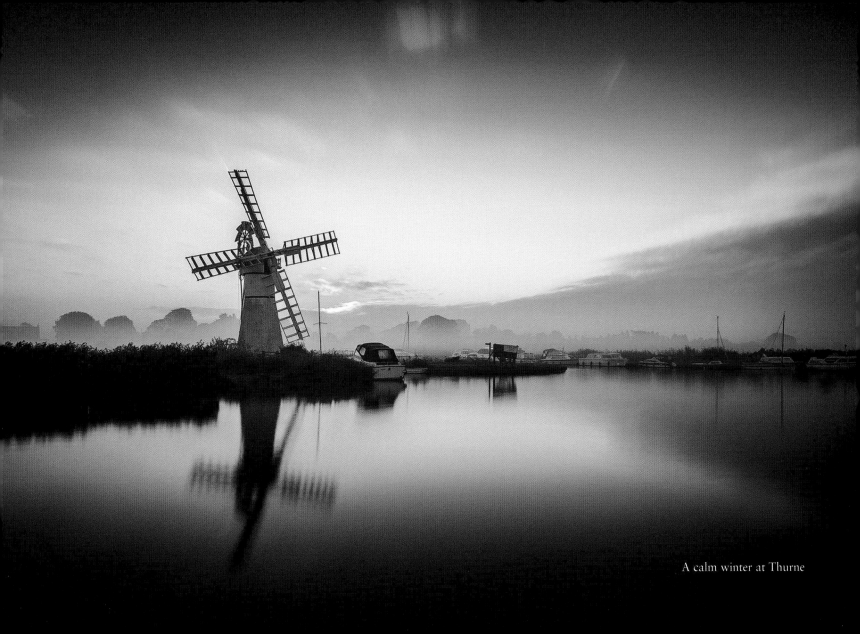

A calm winter at Thurne

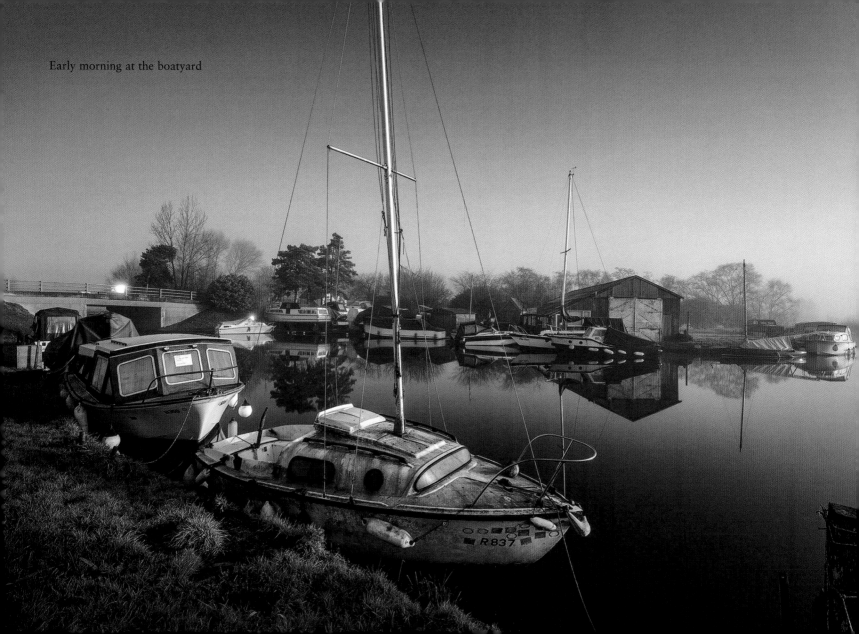

Early morning at the boatyard

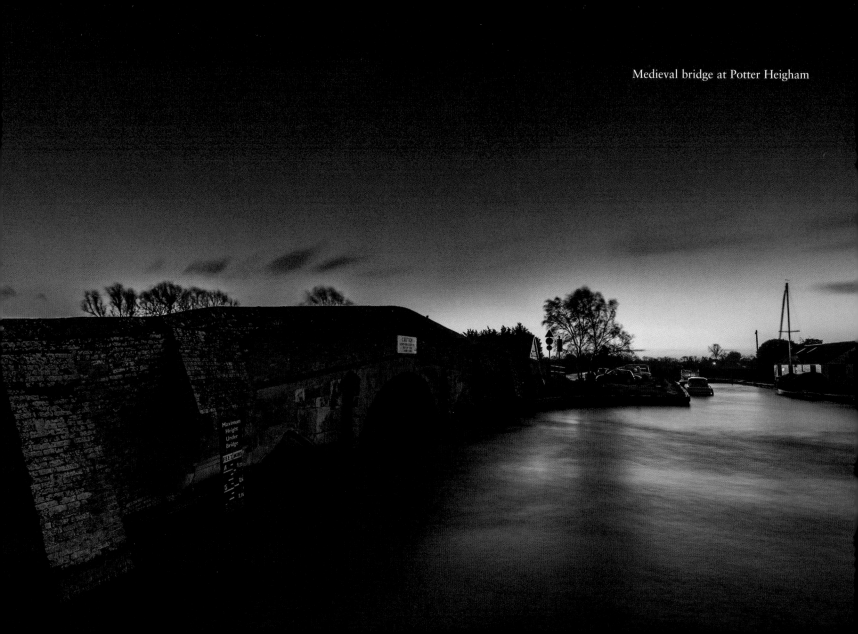

Medieval bridge at Potter Heigham

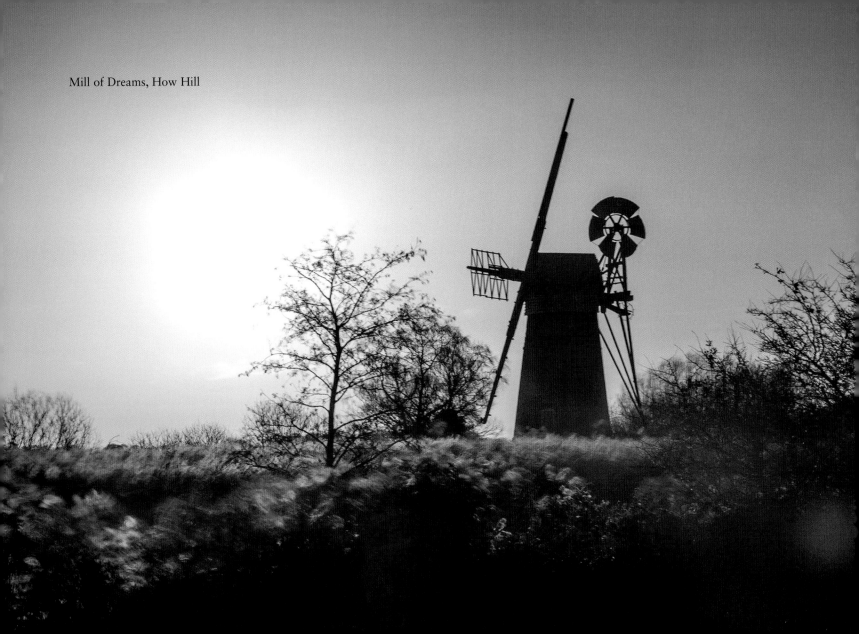

Mill of Dreams, How Hill

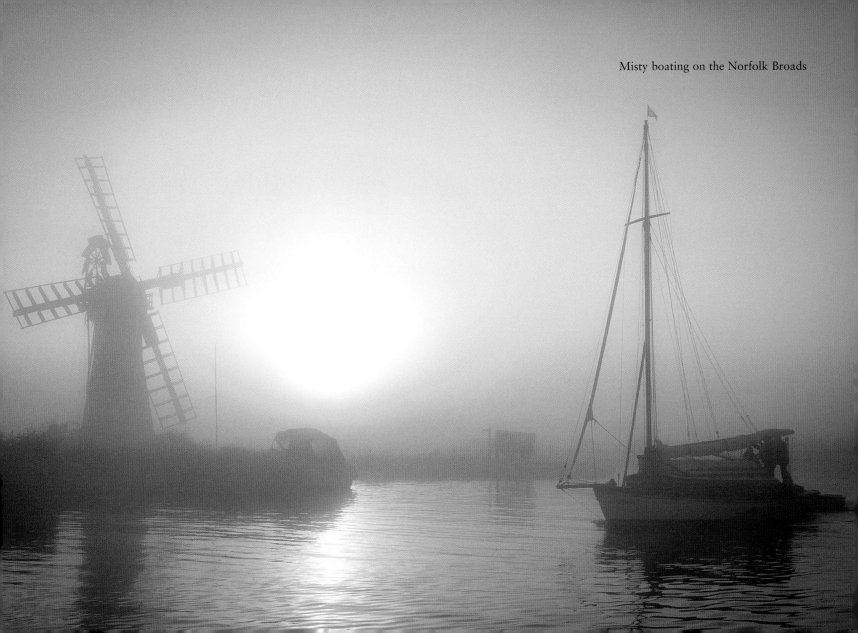

Misty boating on the Norfolk Broads

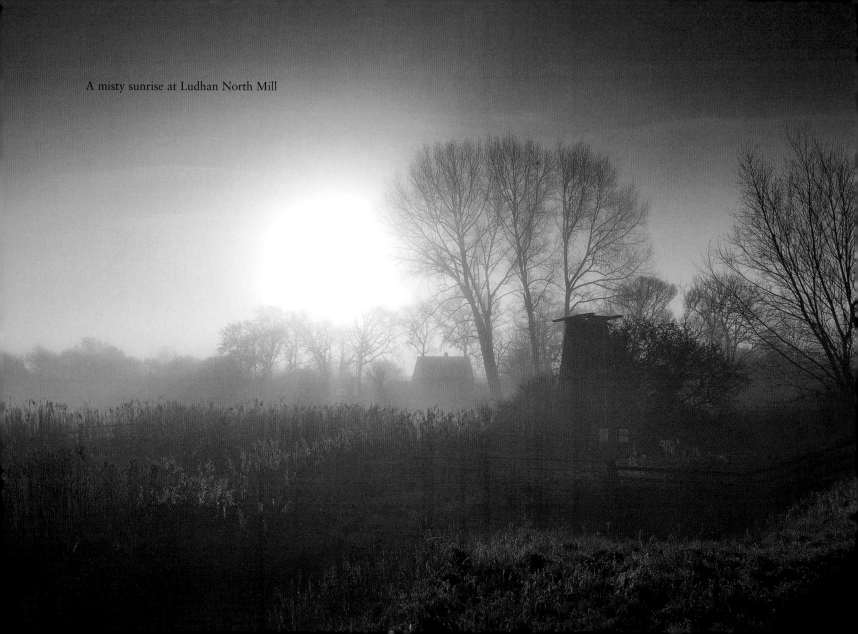

A misty sunrise at Ludhan North Mill

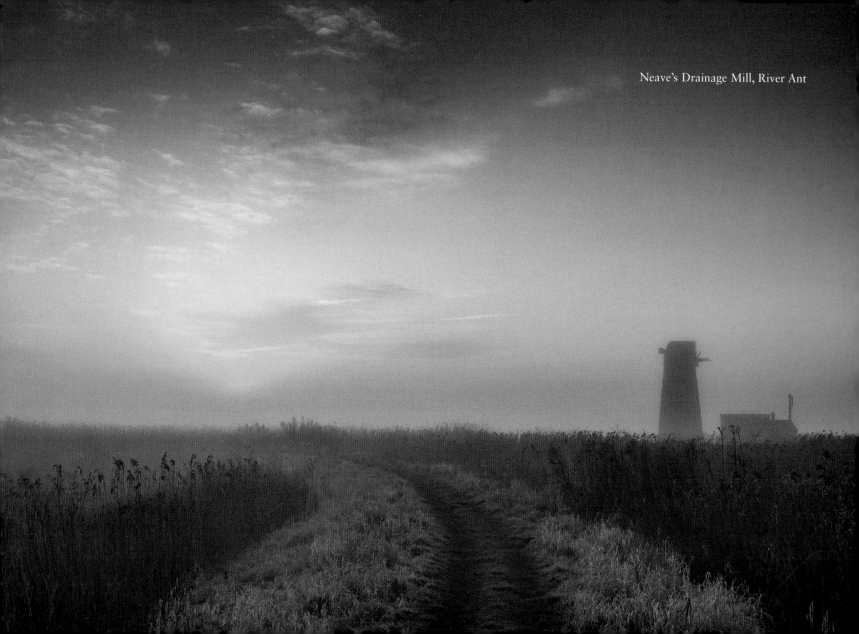

Neave's Drainage Mill, River Ant

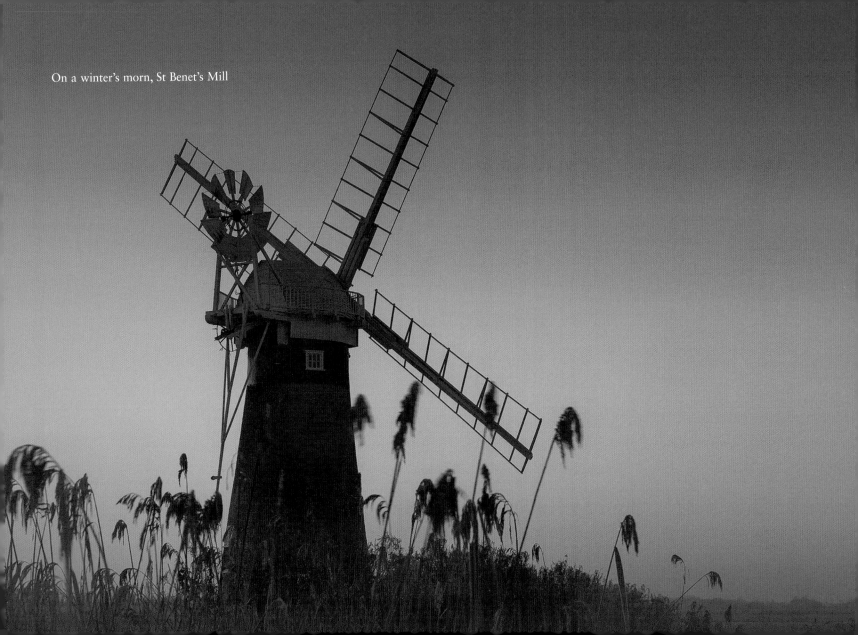

On a winter's morn, St Benet's Mill

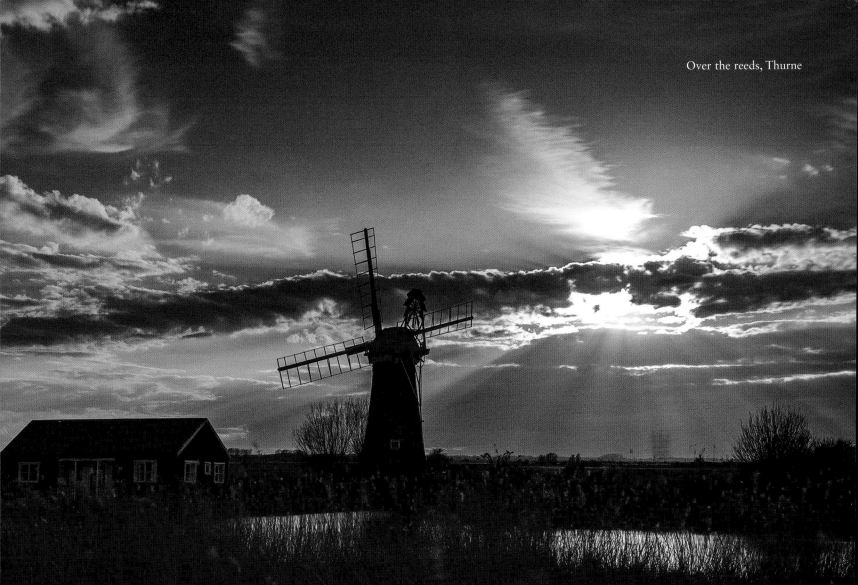

Over the reeds, Thurne

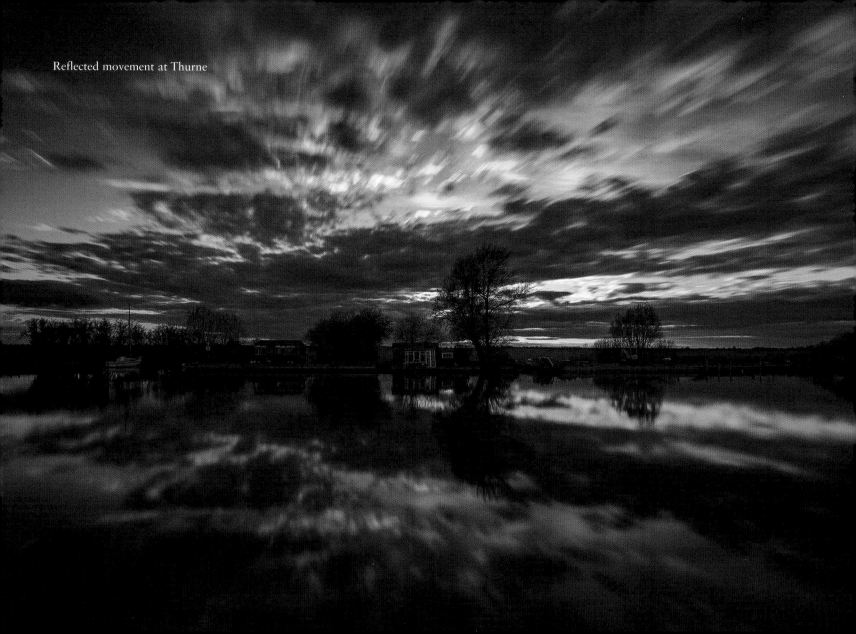

Reflected movement at Thurne

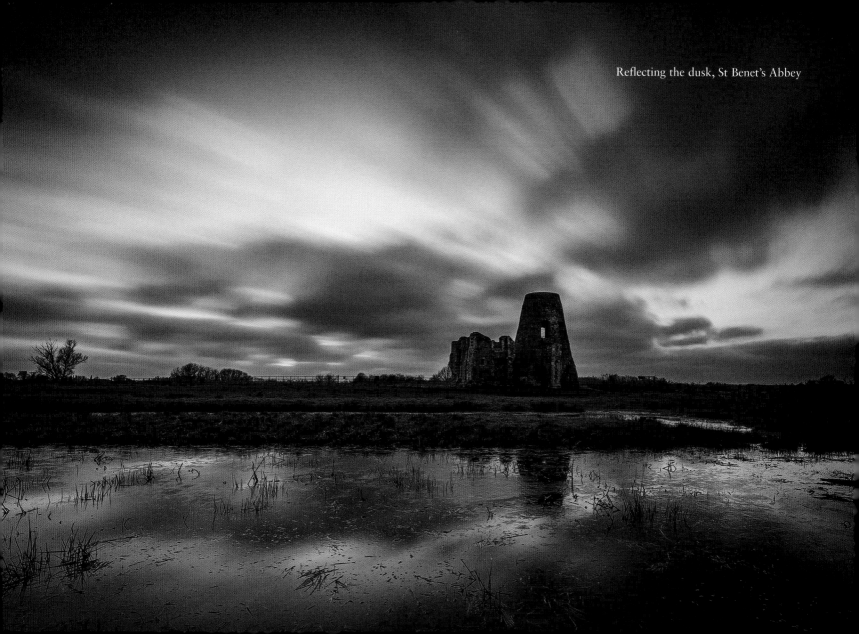

Reflecting the dusk, St Benet's Abbey

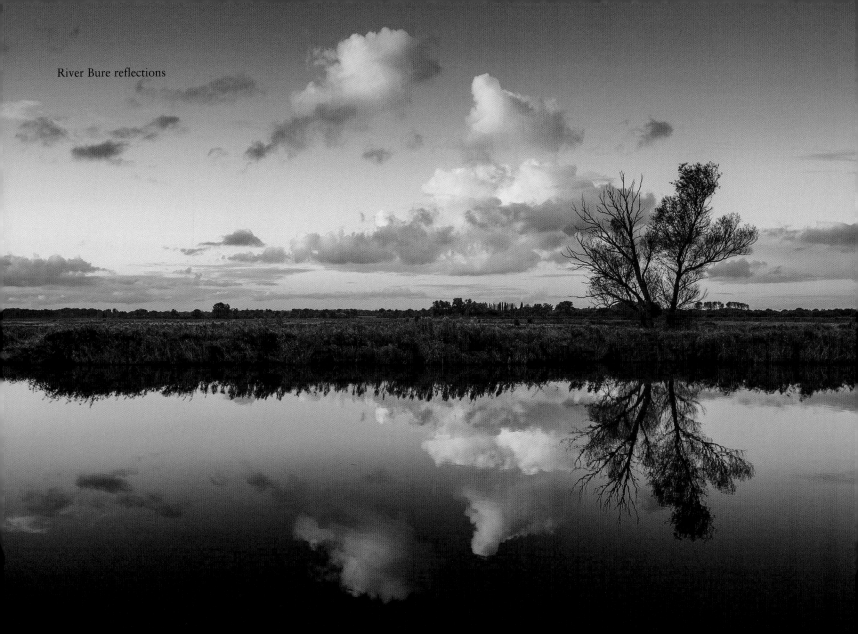

River Bure reflections

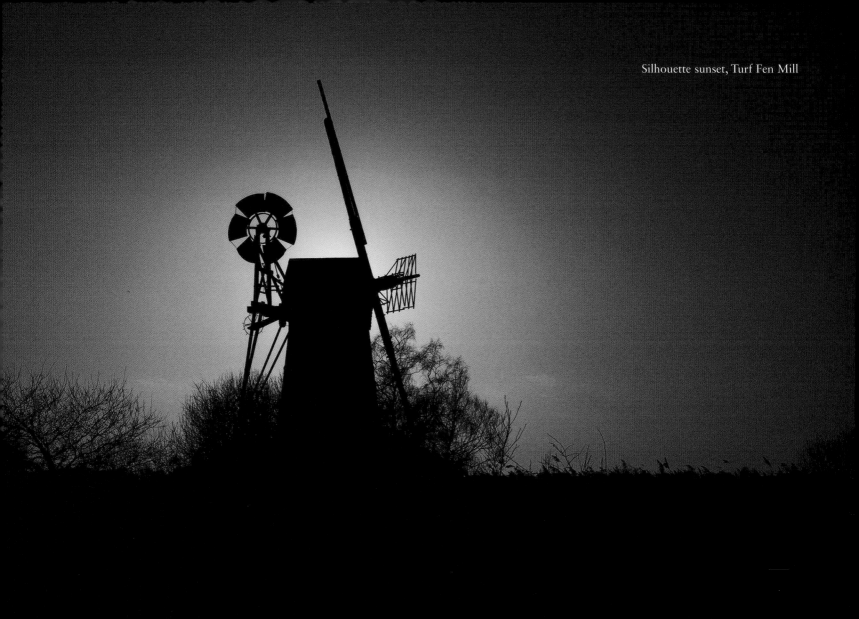

Silhouette sunset, Turf Fen Mill

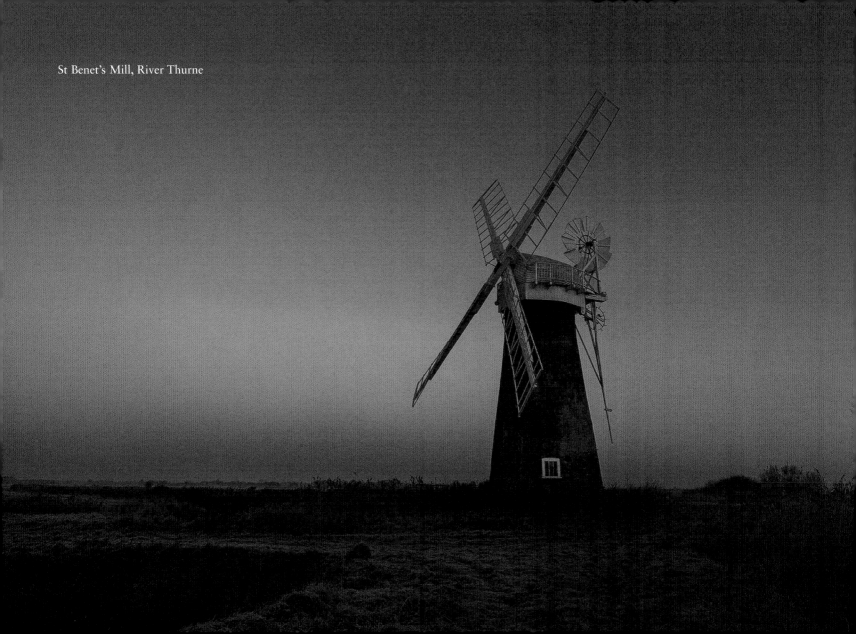

St Benet's Mill, River Thurne

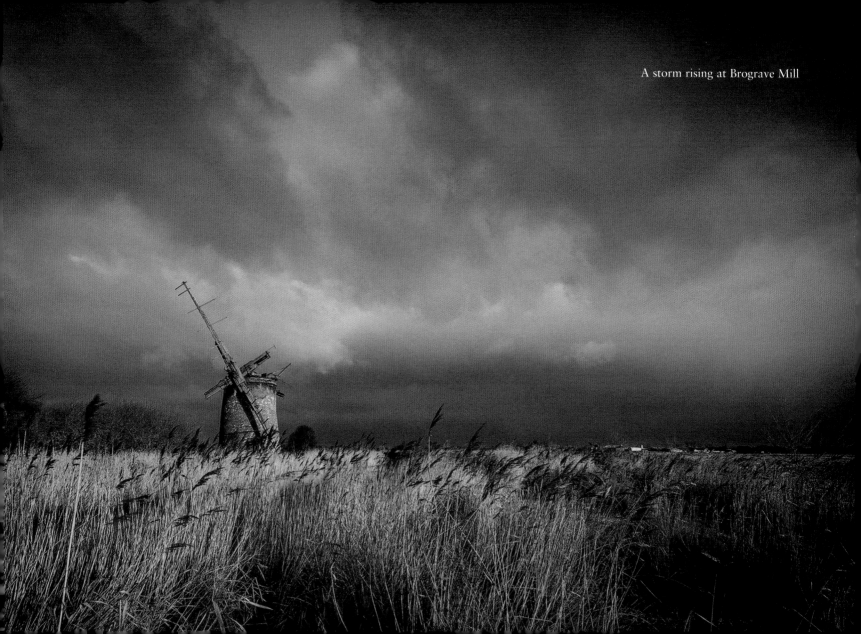

A storm rising at Brograve Mill

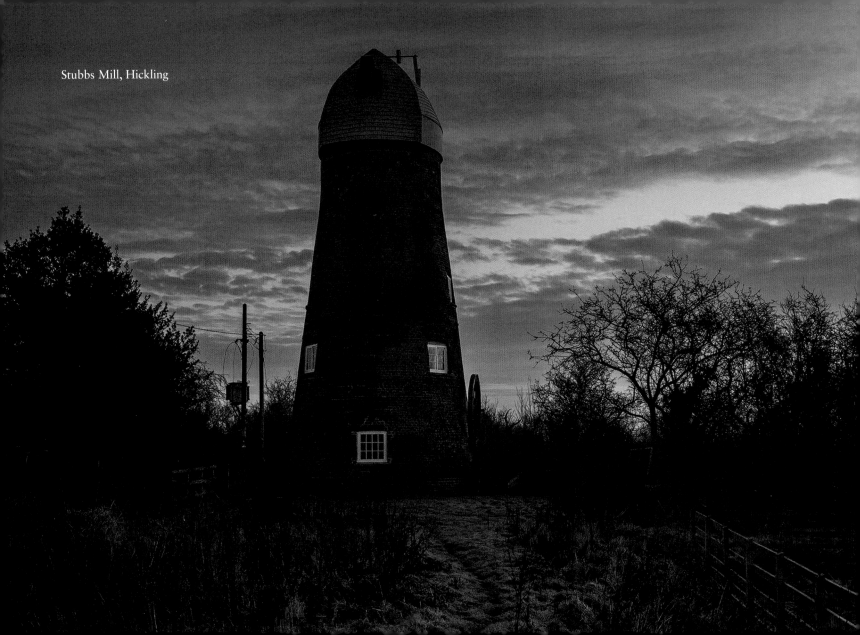

Stubbs Mill, Hickling

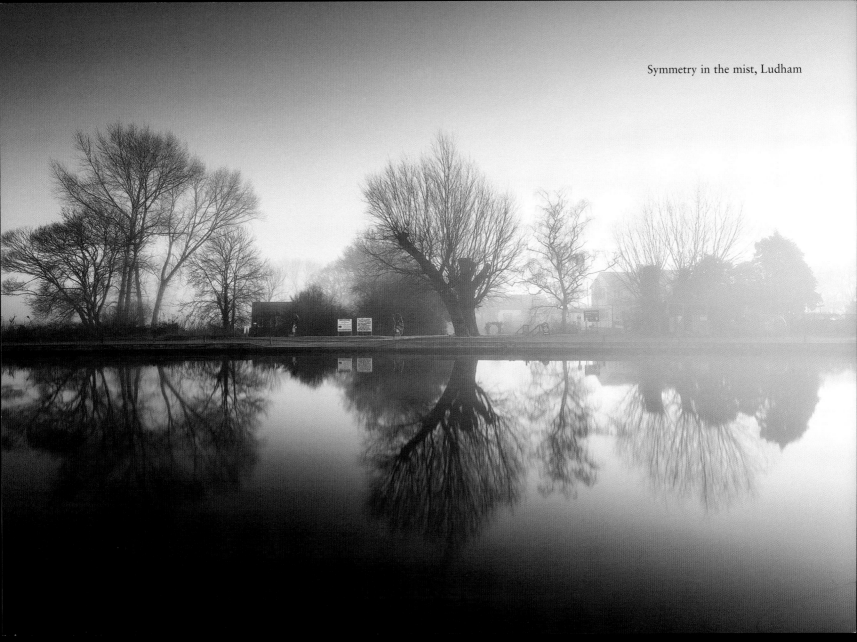

Symmetry in the mist, Ludham

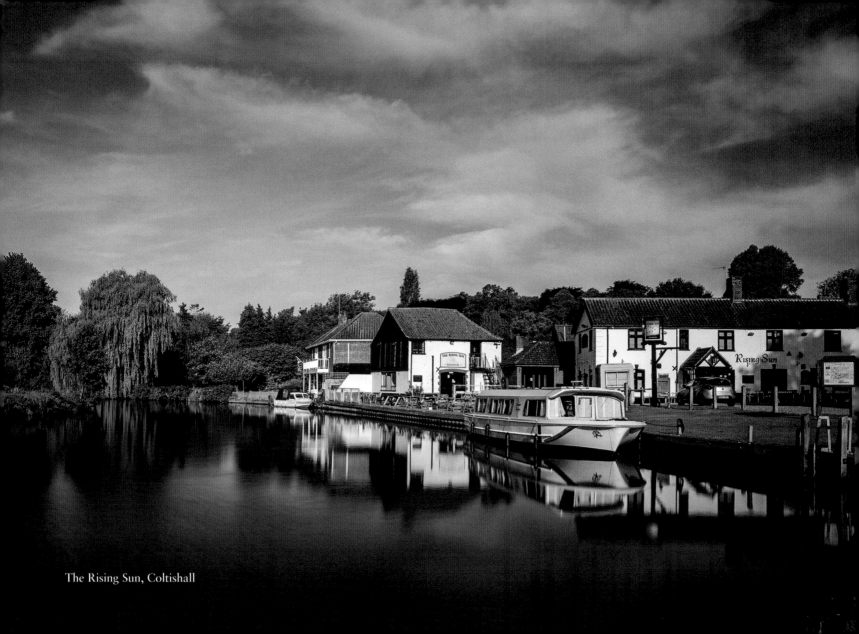

The Rising Sun, Coltishall

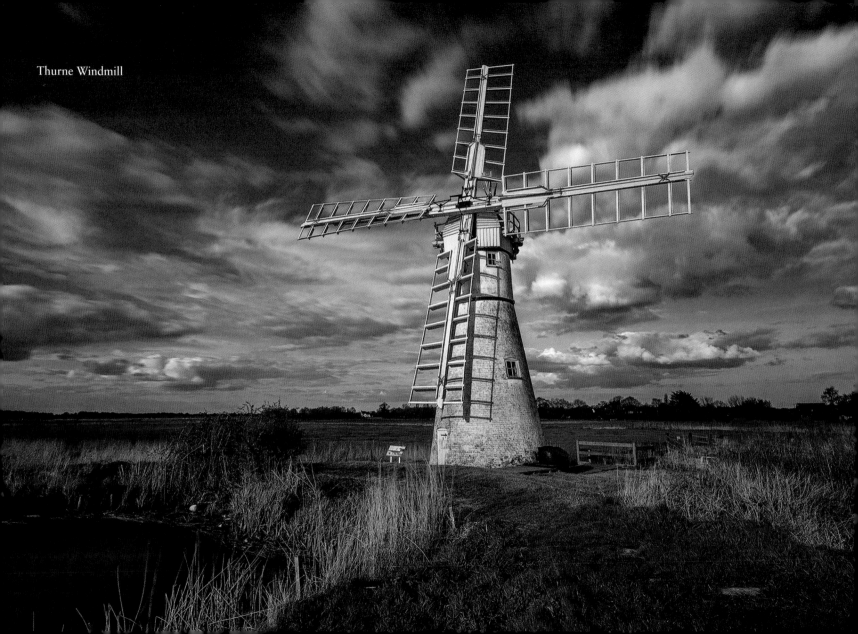

Thurne Windmill

Ludham Bridge

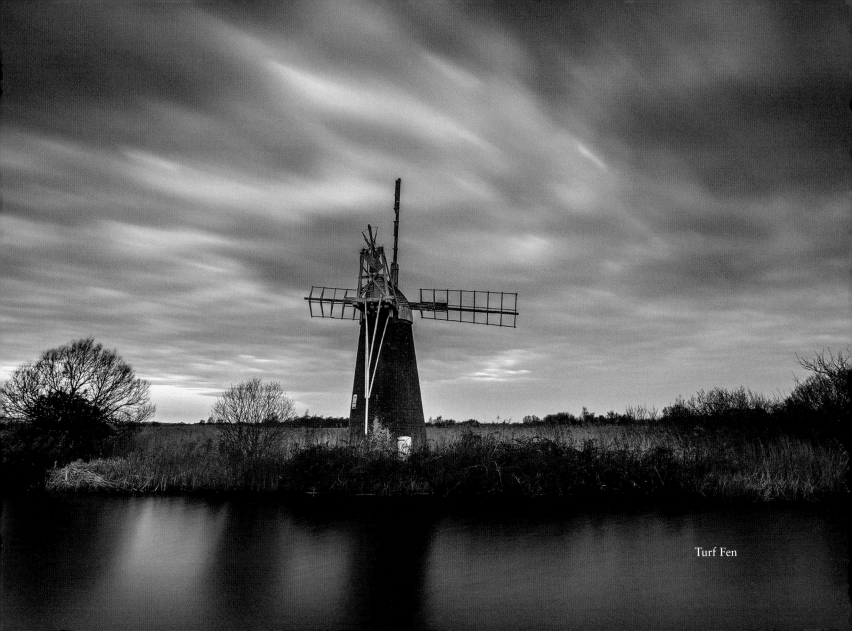

Turf Fen

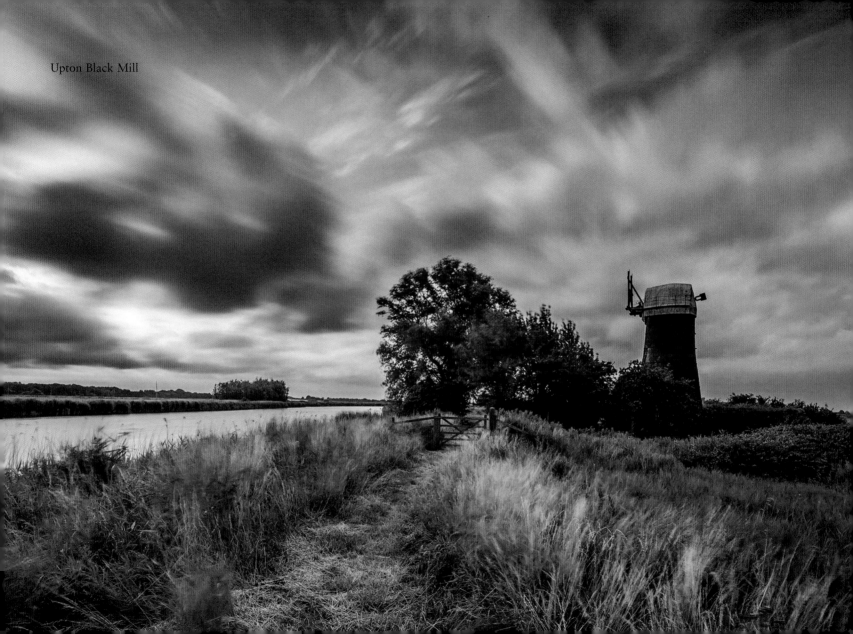

Upton Black Mill

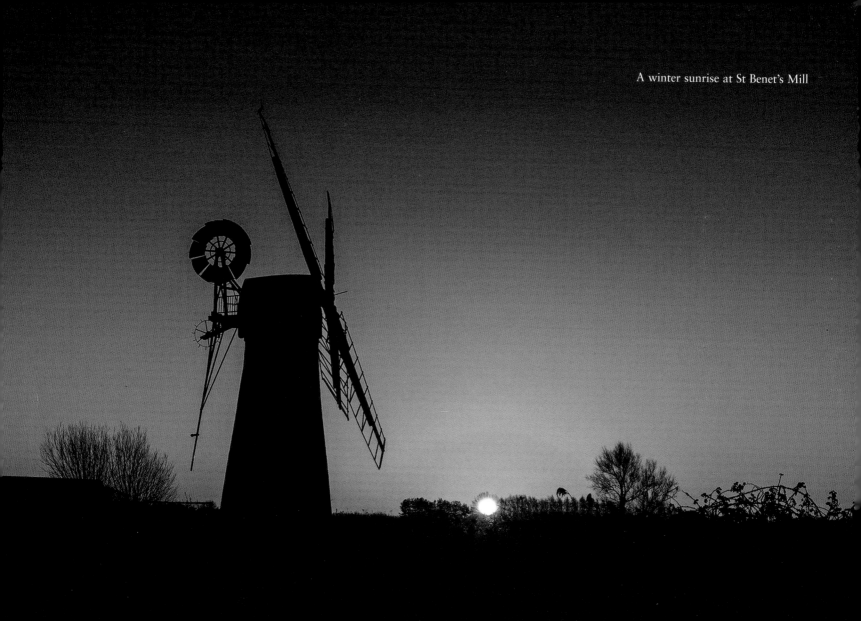

A winter sunrise at St Benet's Mill

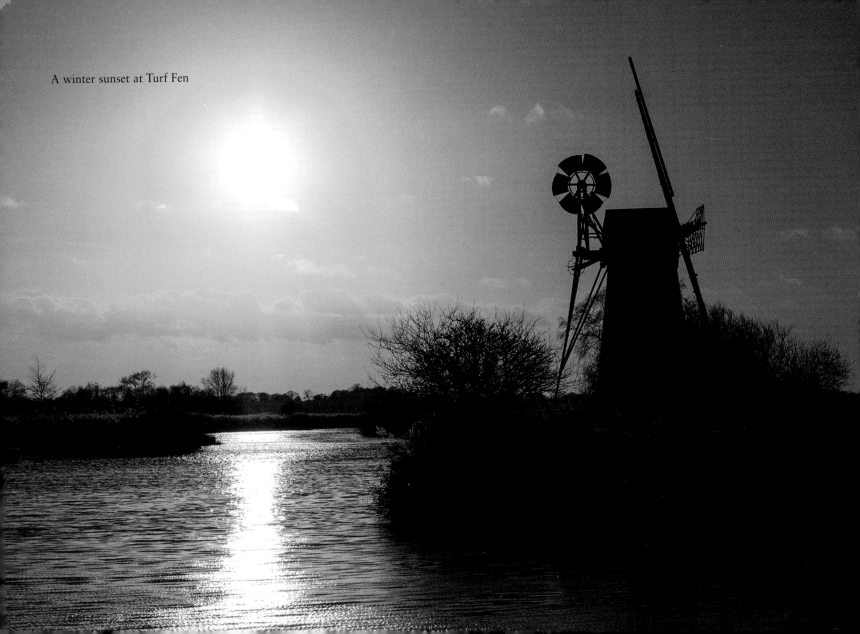

A winter sunset at Turf Fen